SEEK GOD EVERYWHERE

ALSO BY ANTHONY DE MELLO

SEEK GOD EVERYWHERE

REFLECTIONS ON THE
SPIRITUAL EXERCISES OF
St. Ignatius

Anthony de Mello, S.J.

Edited by
Gerald O'Collins, S.J., Daniel Kendall, S.J.,
and Jeffrey LaBelle, S.J.

IMAGE/DOUBLEDAY
New York London Toronto Sydney Auckland

IMAGE

Copyright © 2010 by Society of Jesus, Bombay (Mumbai)
Province

Published in the United States by Doubleday Religion, an
imprint of the Crown Publishing Group, a division of Random
House, Inc., New York.
www.crownpublishing.com

IMAGE, the Image colophon, and DOUBLEDAY are registered
trademarks of Random House, Inc.

Library of Congress Cataloging-in-Publication Data
De Mello, Anthony, 1931–1987
  Seek God everywhere: reflections on the spiritual exercises of
St. Ignatius / by Anthony de Mello; edited by Gerald O'Collins,
Daniel Kendall, and Jeffrey LaBelle.—1st ed.
      p.   cm.
  1. Ignatius, of Loyola, Saint, 1491–1556. Exercitia spiritualia.
2. Spiritual exercises.   3. Spiritual direction.—Christianity.
4. Spiritual life.—Catholic Church.   5. Spirituality.—
Catholic Church.   6. Catholic Church.—Doctrines.   I.
O'Collins, Gerald.   II. Kendall, Daniel.   III. LaBelle, Jeffrey.
IV. Title.
BX2179.L8D38 2009
248.3.—dc22   2009024705

ISBN 978-0-385-53176-4

PRINTED IN THE UNITED STATES OF AMERICA

10 9 8 7 6 5 4 3 2 1

First Edition

Seek God everywhere, so that the whole world

becomes charged with the presence of the beloved.

— ANTHONY DE MELLO

CONTENTS

INTRODUCTION

For all those who cherish the legacy of Father Anthony de Mello, S.J. (1931–1987), this book reveals and presents something that has so far been missing in his published works: the wellspring of his own spiritual life. For Tony de Mello, making the Spiritual Exercises of St. Ignatius Loyola (1491–1556) for himself, directing those doing the Exercises, and teaching others to become skilled directors of the Exercises was the heart of the matter—his specifically Jesuit way to God.

In 1973 de Mello founded near Pune, India, the Sadhana ("Way to God") Institute, a center for training spiritual guides and directors of "retreats," a place to lead those who withdraw from their normal occupations for days or weeks of solitude and intense prayer. The third Sadhana Group consisted of seven Jesuit priests and seven religious sisters.

From July to November 1975, de Mello began the course for that group by lecturing on the Spiritual Exercises. Two or three times a week he gave hour-long talks that were taped. Several members of the group then typed out the talks and gave the others a carbon copy. Thirty years later one of the participants, Father Albert Menezes, S.J., made his copy available to us.

The pages were difficult to read: the typists had frequently used old ribbons, adopted single spacing throughout, and left very little room for margins. In any case a tropical climate had played havoc with the paper. There was no chance of scanning the text and transferring it directly to a computer. A grant from the Jesuit Foundation of the University of San Francisco enabled us to have the pages retyped entirely as a computer document.

Then we faced the task of editing the material. While preserving as much as possible the words and conversational style of de Mello, we have inserted headings and set his talks out in readable paragraphs. He did not always follow the order of the *Spiritual Exercises*. Hence we have, where necessary, rearranged the chapters to follow the order of the Exercises themselves. We have also added endnotes to clarify terminology: for instance, the terms Jesuits apply to their superior general in Rome ("the general"), their superiors in various parts of the world ("the provincials"), and students in training ("the scholastics"). We needed to explain as well some Indian and psychological terms. In particular, the talks of de Mello, himself a trained psychotherapist, adapted occasionally the language of transactional analysis ("parent," "child," and "adult"). Transactional analysis is an integrative approach to the theory of psychology and psychotherapy.

Perhaps the most time-consuming part in editing this manuscript consisted of verifying and giving precise references to different authors, both ancient and modern, when de Mello cited them. Here and there we inserted references and augmented the text with information to make

his writing accessible to a wider audience. Bible quotations
will reflect the New Revised Standard Version style.

For those not familiar with the Exercises, let us explain
briefly what they are and how they work. The man who
would become Ignatius of Loyola and the founder of the
Society of Jesus (the Jesuits), was born Iñigo, the youngest
of the thirteen children of Don Beltrán Yañez de Oñez y
Loyola and Marina Saenz de Lieona y Balda, in the castle of
Loyola in the Basque town of Azpeitia, about forty miles
southwest of Hendaye, the most southwesterly town in
France. He changed his baptismal name, Iñigo, to Ignatius
many years later when living in Rome.

In his early years he did not have much formal education,
yet at the age of sixteen he became a page to Juan Velásquez
de Cuellar, the treasurer of the kingdom of Castile. When
Velásquez died in 1517, Ignatius joined the army. In 1521,
while defending the town of Pamplona against some French
invaders, he was hit with a cannonball, which wounded one
of his legs and broke the other. For the rest of his life he
would walk with a limp.

During his convalescence he read *The Golden Legend*, a
popular collection of lives of the saints, and a *Life of Christ* by
Ludolph the Carthusian. Reflecting quietly on the material
provided by these books and on his own reactions to the reading, he experienced a profound conversion. The questions he
put to himself and the spiritual experiences he underwent
during his convalescence would appear years later in the
pages of his *Spiritual Exercises*. Ignatius's book may be, as de
Mello remarks, "very dry reading" and not normal "spiritual

reading," but the *Spiritual Exercises* come right out of the saint's experience. "He tells you what to do," de Mello adds, "and how to go about doing it. When you practice it, then you will see what he is talking about. You need to experience it for yourself."

After his conversion, Ignatius traveled to the Holy Land in 1523, then gathered a group of companions around him, and afterward studied with them for a number of years at the University of Paris, where he earned his master's degree in 1535. Even though he wouldn't found the Jesuits, or the Society of Jesus, until 1540, Ignatius spent nearly twenty years, between 1523 and 1541, crafting the Spiritual Exercises, directing people in them, and encouraging his followers to do the same.

The purpose of the Exercises is to find the will of God for one's life and to receive insight and encouragement in following one's personal call. The text itself offers guidance for those directing people making the Exercises. As de Mello observes, Ignatius's manual "is like a cookery book. There is nothing drier than a cookery book. But if you put all the ingredients together in the proper proportions, you will produce results." Even for those who are not directors of a retreat, the *Spiritual Exercises* is a wealthy collection of spiritual insight that Jesuits and laypeople have used for hundreds of years.

After proposing a prologue (the "First Principle and Foundation"), Ignatius divides the Exercises into four parts or "weeks." These "weeks" can vary in length and do not necessarily consist of seven days. During the "first week" those making the Exercises meditate on sin and its consequences, with the aim of experiencing a deep repentance or total turning to God. During the "second week" the contemplations and meditations focus on the life of Jesus Christ. Ignatius includes during the second week (1) an "Introduction to the Consideration of Different States of Life"; (2) a "Meditation on the Two Standards" (Does the retreatant really want to serve under the standard of Christ and not that of satan?); (3) a Meditation on "Three Classes of People" (What are three different ways for finding spiritual freedom and choosing which is better?); and (4) a consideration of "Three Degrees of Humility" (How far will a person go in being entirely conformed to the will of Christ?).

The "third week" turns to contemplate Christ's Passion and Death, and in the "fourth week" those making the Exercises contemplate his Resurrection and risen life. The final exercise is called the "Contemplation to Attain the Love of God" (the goal being to receive the grace of "finding God in all things").

To help the directors, Ignatius adds lengthy instructions or guidelines ("Annotations," as they were traditionally called); "Additions" or "additional directions"; and various notes and rules—above all the "Rules for the Discernment of Spirits" (see chapter 7).

The full course of Spiritual Exercises is made over a period of around thirty days and can be adapted, abbreviated, or lengthened, according to how much time people can devote to them, how fast one makes progress, and so on. Ignatius believed that the Exercises in their entirety should be made only once or twice in a person's lifetime.

In the more than 450 years since the Spiritual Exercises came into existence, innumerable people have made them and many authors have written about them. Every Jesuit is required to make them fully at least twice: when he enters the Society and then some years later (usually between ten and twenty years) when his spiritual formation has been completed. Since individual Jesuits come from and live in almost all parts of the world, their own personal and cultural contexts affect the way they approach the Spiritual Exercises. In this book both an Indian and an international perspective come through. Let us next indicate something of the emphases, imaginative suggestions, and particular "take" on the Exercises that color the lectures de Mello gave to his Sadhana Group.

In his opening lectures (from which we continue to quote in this introduction), de Mello comments on the "Annotations," or introductory guidelines for anyone directing or doing the Exercises. The overriding aim is to make a journey through prayer and self-awareness that provides a context for becoming spiritually free and so able to seek, find, and follow the will of God in one's personal life. Such a process of "putting order into our lives," de Mello reflects, "really means putting order into our love." "To love anyone or anything apart from God or as equal to God" is "inordinate; it has to be changed and purified." "We were created for God," de Mello insists. "Our eternal destiny is God; our hearts find rest only in God. Total satisfaction is achieved only in the infinite love of God."

Hence de Mello can call the Exercises "a crash-program for centering our hearts on God." They enable us to let God, and no "created thing on earth," become and remain the "center of gravity" for our lives. Characteristically, it is through a parable that de Mello illustrates this shift of gravity.

De Mello imagines an Indian girl called Mary. She

has a number of loves: she loves her parents very deeply; she loves her friends, her hobbies, and all sorts of other things. Then she falls madly in love with John, and he becomes everything to her. Does this stop her loving her parents and her friends, or does she lose interest in her work and hobbies? No, a new kind of life comes into all of this, and it is obviously charged with the intense love she now has for John. One day John's bosses transfer him to Africa. Mary has the choice of either remaining here in India or going with him. There is no doubt in her mind; she will go to Africa. What will she feel? Will she feel sad leaving her parents? Very much so. She will feel sad for days on end; yet there is not the slightest doubt in her mind what she should do. What has happened to Mary? Her love for her parents has to some extent becomes *relativized* by her love for John. The new dimension in her love does not at all mean that she loses her humanity and her warmth. But somehow her other loves are transformed and given a new center of gravity.

The "spiritual love" encouraged by the Exercises does not mean, de Mello explains, "that we should give up all other loves." Rather we should "move the center of gravity of our hearts onto Christ, and then all the rest become relative." "Attachments," he adds, are not evil; "they are both good and necessary. They become disordered when they become the center of our universe. No attachment to anything created may ever be the center of our loves. When we experience this centering on God, then everything else becomes relativized."

Right from the outset de Mello highlights in his lectures the indispensable role of *interior freedom* in enabling our love to be centered on God and our will to choose what God truly wants from us. "People," he says, "come to a right decision only when their hearts are free." When we are truly free, God can attract our will to what is genuinely for our best and for his greater glory.

As much or even more than Ignatius, de Mello stresses the *roles of silence and solitude* as conditions for such spiritual growth. "Silence," he assures his Sadhana Group, "is the greatest treasure we have." Silence can be "painful," but it brings "purification" and allows us to confront ourselves and God. Through silence we "come in touch" with God. "In that sense, everything is found in silence."

Like Ignatius, de Mello treats the Exercises as "essentially activity. The one thing retreatants must do is to work. Come to the retreat and work hard. In this way it is similar to a Buddhist retreat. Work, work, work, and do not sit down and listen to a retreat master." De Mello warns against doing much reading, "because reading can serve as a pretty good defense against God. When you are wrestling with God and grappling with the state you are in, reading can be a nice anesthetic. A person takes a book and reads in the way a husband reads his newspaper during breakfast so that he will not need to talk to his wife. Reading is a nice defense. Such people are reading all about God, but are not exposing themselves to him."

Likewise, de Mello joins Ignatius in urging fidelity to one's program of prayer on a retreat: "Fix the time and stick to it." He will have none of the idea of "I pray when I feel like it," and argues on the basis of his experience: "It is precisely when people do not feel like praying that they can make great progress in prayer." He adds:

> Prayer has its ups and downs. Sometimes we feel both disgust and exhilaration. We sometimes feel both within the same hour. Although we have instant coffee and instant tea, there is no such thing as instant prayer, just as there is no such thing as instant love and instant relationship. These things need time. When people relate to God, they must invest time. There is yet another reason for staying when we feel like leaving. The inevitable experience of people who say "I pray when I feel like it" is that they pray less and less. Then they need to start all over again.

Along with this sober advice, de Mello also promises that those who make the Exercises with faithful generosity can be led to mystical experience. An intense, immediate, and deeply consoling communion with God in prayer frequently results from such fidelity.

When in 1975 de Mello gave the talks that make up this book, he used the translation by Louis J. Puhl, S.J., *The Spiritual Exercises of St. Ignatius* (Chicago: Loyola University Press, 1951). Since de Mello delivered his talks in 1975 and, in particular, since his untimely death in 1987, other translations have appeared: for instance, Joseph A. Munitiz and Philip Endean, *Saint Ignatius of Loyola: Personal Writings* (London: Penguin, 1996); and David L. Fleming, *Draw Me into Your Friendship. A Literal Translation and Contemporary Reading of the Spiritual Exercises* (St. Louis: Institute of Jesuit Sources, 1996). Many excellent studies of the Exercises have also been published: for example, James L. Connor et al., *The Dynamism of Desire: Bernard J. F. Lonergan, S.J., on the Spiritual Exercises of Saint Ignatius of Loyola* (St. Louis: Institute of Jesuit Sources, 2006); David L. Fleming, ed., *Notes on the Spiritual Exercises of St. Ignatius of Loyola* (St. Louis: Review for Religious, 1981); and Michael Ivens, *Understanding the Spiritual Exercises* (Leominster, Herefordshire: Gracewing, 1998). To update what de Mello said in his talks, we have at some points introduced endnotes from these and other authors.

We are most grateful to Father Albert Menezes for providing us with his copy of the notes from 1975 and to Francis de Melo, Jesuit Provincial of Bombay, for allowing us to use them. We want to express our deep gratitude to Philip Endean for help in tracing sources used by de Mello and to Father David Fleming, longtime editor of *Review for Religious*, for making very valuable suggestions about editing these talks by de Mello. We are indebted to our literary agent, Mr. Joseph Durepos, and to Gary Jansen of Doubleday for their hard work and expert advice in helping us prepare this manuscript. We have deposited in the Archives of the California Province of the Society of Jesus (1) the original text entrusted to us by Father Albert Menezes, (2) the complete typescript we had made from this text, and (3) our edited version in its first, longer state.

We dedicate this book to the memory of Anthony de Mello, a treasured and delightful companion in the Society of Jesus. An inspiring teacher, for his lectures in 1975 he drew on a wide range of written sources, both primary and secondary, as well as on his own personal experience as a master of the spiritual life. May this book illustrate something very dear to him: the enduring power of the Spiritual Exercises to bring believers everywhere closer to God and to their fellow human beings.

Gerald O'Collins, S.J., Daniel Kendall, S.J., and
  Jeffrey LaBelle, S.J.
July 31, 2009
University of San Francisco

SEEK GOD EVERYWHERE

First Principle and Foundation

*We are created to praise, reverence
and serve God our Lord.*
—IGNATIUS OF LOYOLA

*After citing classical authors who witness to the need for
silence, de Mello expounds on the unique significance of
God. We need to fall in love with the Absolute.*

I would like to make some preliminary remarks on silence
before we talk of the matter at hand. There is a little phrase
from Thomas Merton (1915–1968) that I find very beautiful: "The world of men has forgotten the joys of silence, the
peace of solitude, which is necessary, to some extent, for
the fullness of human living." A few lines later Merton
adds: "Man cannot be happy for long unless he is in contact
with the springs of spiritual life which are hidden in the
depths of his own soul. If man is exiled constantly from his
own home, locked out of his spiritual solitude, he ceases to
be a true person."

There is only one way for people to confront themselves
and that is through silence. All of us need to develop a tol-
erance for silence, a home to ourselves, a place to touch the
wellsprings of life inside of us. There is nothing as valuable

as silence. All of us must go back and be in touch with our inner resources.

There is one passage that I like very much in the Camaldolese *Constitutions* that reads: "We are frequently cast out from our hearts as the sea casts out a dead body." This is very vivid and well described. We go into our hearts and are pushed out. We cannot take it. We cannot stay. We cannot be still. Yet as these *Constitutions* state, "[T]o the quiet and persevering hermit the silence of the cell brings a blessed sweetness and a refreshing sweetness that tastes of paradise." This can be glorious literature for people who want to escape; even so, it is difficult to deny the truth of it.

Thomas Merton quotes a Syrian monk, in his book *Contemplative Prayer*: "If you love truth, be a lover of silence. Silence like the sunlight will illuminate you in God and will deliver you from the phantoms of ignorance. . . . In the beginning we have to force ourselves to be silent. But then there is born something that draws us to silence. . . . If only you practice this, untold light will dawn on you in consequence . . . after a while a certain sweetness is born in the heart of this exercise and the body is drawn almost by force to remain in silence." All the mystics say that once you get acclimated to silence, there is a great sweetness in it.

"Behold my beloved," says Ammonas, a disciple of St. Anthony of the Desert (about 251–356). "I have shown you the power of silence and how fully God dwells in those who remain in silence; it is by silence that the power of God dwells in those saints of the past and so the mysteries of God are known to them."

Kahlil Gibran says: "You talk when you cease to be at peace with your thoughts and when leaving the solitude of your heart you live in your lips and sound becomes a diversion and a pastime."

Even Evelyn Underhill (1875–1941), an outstanding mystic herself, believes that "the self is yet unacquainted with the strange claim of silence which soon becomes familiar to even those who attempt the lowest activities of the contemplative life, where the self is released from succession, the voices of the world are not heard and the great adventures of the soul begin to take place."

Simone Weil (1909–1943), the Jewish mystic, says, "At times the first words [of the Our Father] tear my thoughts from my body and transport me outside space where there is neither perspective nor point of view . . . Filling every part of this infinity of infinity, there is a silence, a silence which is not an absence of sound but which is the object of a positive sensation, more positive than that of sound. Noises, if there are any, only reach me after crossing this silence."

In a sense, silence is God. I love music passionately, but when I am in the mood for silence, even music is too jarring. I want only silence to be present. A person could say that silence is a harmony more beautiful than any other harmony. I think that most people have experienced at least fleeting moments of this. Let me tell you a story.

The day before yesterday I went to say Mass for some people in the seminary. I rose early in the morning and went outside to wait for a group of scholastics [Jesuits in training who have not taken final vows]. It was quite cold. I was looking up at the sky and this thing hit me, this silence. It lasted for about a minute, but I am still experiencing the effects of it. It is the world we know but there is no knowing. We suddenly sense it. Each of us experiences it in different ways.

This morning I was talking to a scholastic while standing under a tree. A bird was chirping. I do not know what kind of bird it was; it sounded like a cuckoo. I supposed it aroused childhood memories in me of forests and similar things. Even when I was talking to him, I sensed that I was listening to what he was saying and yet I was not. I was there but I was not there. After a while I had to say, "Look, let's stop talking because I am not completely here." There was a call to come home, to take myself away from this world. One author puts it well: "Silence is not so much a disciple on the tongue as a disciple on the ear." We keep silence not to stop talking but to open our ears, to perceive something, to sense something. If I say to a group: "Let's keep quiet and listen," we will hear sounds all around—footsteps on the gravel outside on the drive, or the rustling of the wind in the leaves, things that we would not hear if we were talking, talking, talking. Sometimes the silence becomes very deep. Then what I experienced the other morning or this morning when I was with that scholastic, one can pick up suddenly. We must always be silent to pick up something like a flash of the Infinite, of the Eternal.

The "First Principle and Foundation" is unique because it is not an exercise. It was incorporated much later by Ignatius as an introduction before he presented a finalized text to be approved by Pope Paul III. It is not given in the form of an exercise at all. It does not have those famous preludes, petitions, and colloquies. We are not told when to make this exercise or if to make it all, how to do it, and so on. Rather it is a declaration. Ignatius recommends it to people who want light exercises. Most people who were giving retreats under his direction would use it as a kind of touchstone to test the retreatants. Were they ready to make the thirty-day exercises? They would tell the retreatants: "This is where I am going to lead you. Are you ready to come?"

The "First Principle and Foundation" is a beautiful statement: "Man is created to praise, reverence, and serve God our Lord, and by this means to save his soul." Where will you find people who have incorporated it into their lives? If a retreatant said: "I would like to be this kind of person," Ignatius would reply, "Let us begin so that by the end of the second week you will be this kind of person." What kind of persons are these people? They are those who really have their goal in view. They know exactly for what they were created, and they will use the whole of creation to attain that goal. Everything else is rigorously subordinated to that desire, whether it be death or life, poverty or riches, honor or dishonor, health or sickness. What does it matter? Everything else is very secondary. The main focus is the goal for which we were created: *to praise, reverence, and serve God our Lord.*

However, in my own experience this approach creates problems for people today. I remember years ago, when I was giving retreats in the Far East, I only had to say we were created for God and, at that point, eight or so men walked out emotionally and one did so physically. How could we believe that we were created for God? Even a person like Louis Evely (1910–1985) attacked the whole idea of the "First Principle and Foundation" as ridiculous, unchristian, and pagan. All that Evely wrote is true, but only partially true. The first sentence about the human being "created to praise, reverence, and serve God our Lord" does not appeal to the modern mind.

This struck me very forcefully when I was talking to a scholastic some time ago. He was telling me how, when he was a regent, he had fallen in love with a woman—actually with more than one—and he was having difficulty in keeping them apart. He needed to be careful that one would not know about the other and all the rest of it. When he was describing the situation to me he said: "This is the time when I forgot I was a Jesuit, I forgot God, I forgot prayer and the Mass. I would go to Mass but the whole experience was so empty. The only thing that mattered was Mary. If I did not see her one day, I was miserable; if I would see her, everything was great. If the phone rang and I was told, 'There is a call for you,' I would go just to hear Mary's voice."

I had an image of him standing near the phone, and when he heard Mary's voice, he brightened up. He was all alive when he encountered her. When he could not talk to her, he was crushed. He was a poor man, withdrawn, being thrown up and down on the waves of his emotions, completely helpless, powerless, living very superficially, and going through the agonies of relating. What is life and what is love if that is all there is to it?

To be thrilled by another human person, to be crushed by the rejection of another person, moving up and down or moving from one person to another, or holding to one person, being completely committed but never having anything of a wider vision and nothing else—is this what life is about? When existentialists consider this situation, they say that this is the great superficiality of human life. Jean-Paul Sartre (1905–1980), for instance, keeps repeating again and again: "We want to anesthetize ourselves; we do not want to realize that underneath all of this there is nothingness. When we realize that, the only proper attitude is despair and tremendous anxiety." The great superficiality of human life! We usually do not go deeper. I think that if people went deeper, they would find the Absolute, the Eternal where they are finally anchored.

I contrast this to an image of a Rishi there on a Himalayan mountain, waking up in the morning and waiting for the rising sun in adoration and reverence. There is a rising sun within his heart! He is in touch with the Absolute and has complete serenity and peace. He has found that since it is true that God exists, then nothing else exists. If it is true that God is good, then what Jesus said to the rich man is true (Luke 18:22–24); namely, that he had to give up all his riches to enter the kingdom. In this way, he can realize his utter dependence upon the Absolute, that "[n]o one is good but God alone" (Luke 18:19).

If it is true that there is an Absolute, then all the rest is shadow. There are images, it is true, but then our reality is relative reality. For example, we do not fall in love with a letter. Just yesterday I was reading a book, *The Intimate Enemy*, where the author says that some have the knack to fall in love not with people but with their letters. I fall in love with the letter you wrote to me, and you fall in love with the letter I wrote to you—a kind of love at a distance. It turns out that I am in love with your letters and do not even know you. It could be that I am all taken up with an image or photograph of you, but I am not in touch with your living, vibrant self. The secret of human life is not falling in love with illusion. The ultimate meaning of human life is to get in touch with the Absolute, to discover the Absolute, to achieve fusion, union with the Absolute.

Then everything else makes sense, everything falls into place.

Charles de Foucauld, who had been an atheist for a long time, put it very nicely when he said: "When I came to know that God exists I could do nothing but live for him." He continued: "It is like eternal beauty, eternal goodness, infinite goodness, infinite loveliness; that is the end of it. I am captivated; so do not entertain me with relative reality." He then went on to assert: "We shall be detached from all ideas by banishing every memory, every knowledge, every bit of thought that God does not make it a duty for us to keep, and remember only Jesus, think only of Jesus. Consider any curiosity an asset against his love and deem as gain any loss through which a greater place is made for Jesus, compared with whom everything else is as nothing." This may sound scandalous, but this is what Paul says in Philippians 3:6–8; namely, that everything is garbage . . . he deems everything as loss, and he did in fact lose everything in order to gain the knowledge of Jesus Christ, his Lord. This is also very similar to Ignatius when he says: "Man is created to praise, reverence, and serve God our Lord."

All the mystics, even Teilhard, say the same thing. Teilhard says, and no one would accuse him of not being incarnational enough, that if all we want is love, we have many people who love us so tenderly, so passionately, so completely, people to whom we can give our hearts. But he also says, addressing himself to Jesus, that it is not enough for him to have someone to love. He needs from the very depths of his being someone to adore. He needs adoring love or loving adoration and this no one can supply except You. In another place he says that mankind will soon have to make a choice between total suicide—or biological suicide—and adoration. In other words, humans must find the Absolute, the *object* of adoration. If they do not find the Absolute, then they are headed for destruction, for meaninglessness, for loss of appetite for life.

Jesus wants people to approach the kingdom with this disposition. Do they approach a retreat with this same disposition when they stand before the kingdom and say that they will sell everything to get this precious pearl, everything? This is the kind of attitude we are talking about. This is what Ignatius is inviting us to in the "First Principle and Foundation."

FALLING IN LOVE WITH THE ABSOLUTE

There is not a single good thing that cannot be perverted. To put it in the language of the great mystics such as St. John of the Cross and others, there is not a single grace of God that the devil cannot use to his own purposes, or that the devil cannot counterfeit. Look at the parable of the weeds and the wheat (Matt. 13:25–30). When both sprout up, they look the same, but one can be dangerous and the other is not. Likewise, falling in love with the Absolute is both beautiful and dangerous. Do we become completely otherworldly? Do we fall in love with the Absolute and neglect relative reality? No.

How can deeply spiritual people—people who are absolutely in love with God and with the Absolute reality, people who are living radically for God—be impossible to live with? What is their main problem? The majority of their problems are not spiritual; the problems do not come from the fact that people are not in love with the Absolute. They have human problems that result from not becoming human enough; they are not able to love enough; they cannot relate well. Here we see two extremes. One is this: "Let us fall in love with the Absolute. What does the rest matter?" As a result such people live loveless, lonely lives as far as other human beings are concerned. The other extreme is, as someone rather sarcastically said, "We are all lovey-dovey and now we are going to bleed over each other. We are going to live for one another—this is the only reality." Such people are completely ignorant of the silence of the Eternal and the Absolute all around them. They are like children playing games and are not aware of the mighty backdrop behind these games. As a result they are impoverished and superficial. The solution? To combine the two.

We might see people whom we love and limit ourselves only to them. For instance, I might believe that here is someone whom I love very deeply, with all my heart. This is meaningless, however, unless I see him or her in God. This type of love can be poor, very transitory, quite ephemeral, too little, and superficial. When I see another person in the context of God, when I see his or her loveliness as a reflection of God, when I can see the loveliness in the context of eternal loveliness and beauty, and when I give my whole heart and soul to the other within this context, then it is complete. We can compare this to music. We might tell ourselves: "How beautiful this note is when it is heard within the whole symphony." We do not want it to be sharp or flat when it is supposed to be a natural note. Likewise, if the note is perfect, it is only so within the context of the symphony. Let me give an example for our consideration. Some people have impaired bodily faculties: Their senses do not function, they have poor health in general, but they live joyfully and happily. I encourage them to see a doctor and I urge them to get help to improve their vision, improve their hearing, improve their overall being, and to live more fully, to live more healthily. On the other hand we might find a man who is totally dedicated to the cult of his body and his faculties. That is all. He is not living; he has missed out on life, and he is only looking after his health. I would prefer those with poor health who are really living and enjoying life rather than this man. This is likely to happen to us if we are so taken up with the reality of this world that we miss out on life by missing out on the Absolute. That is a tremendous loss.

We must have this awareness. If we lack it, then we will not make any headway. We need to have a clear vision, clear as the stars in the sky early in the morning—clear and shining bright. When people realize that this is what I am created for, this is what I want, then everything else falls into perspective. Otherwise things will become confused.

Gandhi's Vision

Gandhi made a statement along this line, and no one can accuse him of not being involved in the modern world. "Man's ultimate aim," said Gandhi, "is the realization that all his activities, social, political, religious, have to be guided to the ultimate aim of the vision of God. The immediate service of all human beings becomes a necessary part of that endeavor simply because the only way to find God is seeing him in his creation and to be one with him."

Gandhi is speaking exactly the same language as Ignatius:

We are all created for the vision of God; everything else is geared to attaining this. "So," Gandhi continues, "I must serve my fellowmen and become one with them. If I could persuade myself that I could find him in a Himalayan cave, I would proceed there immediately, but I know that I cannot find him apart from humanity."

Both things were very clear in his mind: namely, his first and overriding loyalty was to the Absolute. The purpose of identifying with humanity is to find God even though humanity is not God. What clarity of vision Gandhi had! Jesus' clarity of vision led to his Father, and he had come here on earth to take us to his Father.

In another place Gandhi said that truth is God, nothing more and nothing less. Nothing and no one else is. Everything else is illusion: wife, children, friends, possessions, all must be held subject to truth; each one should be sacrificed in the search of God. He could not be more brutal in saying these things. Gandhi also asserted: "I am a humble seeker after truth. I am impatient to realize myself, to attain *moksha* [freedom, salvation] in this very existence; my national service is part of my training for *moksha*. Thus considered, my service may be regarded as pure selfishness, since I have no desire for the perishable things of this earth; I am striving for the kingdom of heaven which is *moksha*." This man was a spiritual giant in his own right. Those who read his writings, quite apart from his politics, have found that they really have the ring of truth, of real experience. I sometimes may disagree with him, but very respectfully. When I disagree I still realize that what he says has the ring of experience and the genuineness of one who has sensed this. All who have discovered the Absolute, who are in love with the Absolute, are firmly convinced that human life is for this, and apart from this it has no meaning.

INDWELLING LOVE

Look at the formula that Ignatius used: "to love everyone in God." We are in danger of falling into one of two extremes: One is to love everyone without loving God; the other is to love God without really loving everyone. It has to be both: "I really love you with love and tenderness and passion; and I really love you in God." If you said: "In loving this person I love God," you are saying something different. There is perhaps a fraction of a millimeter of difference, and yet there is a difference. To discover the difference is difficult. What is it? You might say, "I love Mary, and I love God"—something that is perfectly true. Someone else might say: "I love Mary, and I love Mary with my whole heart, and in loving Mary I love God." That is completely off the track. Perhaps I might say, "I experience the Eternal in my love for Mary." But isn't it first the experience of loving Mary totally, and then the head comes along and says, "This is God"? This is not an experience but a theological reflection. When it is an experience, I might say the exact same thing and truly have the experience.

St. Augustine of Hippo (354–430), St. Thomas Aquinas (around 1225–1274), and others assert that human life would be meaningless if the Eternal and the Infinite did not exist. If it were not for the Eternal, if there were no Infinite, everything would be meaningless. I would despair. In such a case I would agree with the existentialists. We would need to anesthetize ourselves and forget about trying to find the meaning of life; we should just live from moment to moment. If then we were to lapse into silence, begin to go into greater depths and reflect, then we would be struck by the meaninglessness of the whole thing.

It is for this reason that I would like to emphasize the beauty of the Exercises and the defectiveness of the Exercises. They are beautiful because they give this vision to people who make them wholeheartedly. These people are molded into living this vision, which becomes flesh and blood in their lives. The defectiveness is that if people are not alert, their humanity will suffer. They can easily fall into the trap of escapism. They could easily escape from the toils and struggles of relating to people and of being involved with the world. Ignatius himself had achieved the synthesis, although he did not have the theology for it. It is like a love affair between God and the whole of creation.

Let's take an example of an affection that is disordered but not sinful.

You have a million rupees. The first possibility is that you stole them from the poor and therefore to keep them is a grave sin. That is a sinful attachment. The second possibility is that you came by the money by telling a lie that harms no one, a venial sin. If you cling to the money, that is a sinful attachment. If you give it up, however, God will be pleased. If you keep it, God will not be fully pleased even though you are not offending him by keeping the money. If you give it up, you would give him more glory, something that would be more pleasing to him. After knowing that, if you still cling to it, is your attachment sinful? No. It is inordinate. You would rather hold the money than give God greater pleasure. In this case you do not love the money only for God. It is not as if God is your only Master. If his greater glory is the overwhelming good, then you should be ready to give up the money. This is a well-ordered attachment, spiritual love. You love the money with a spiritual love. You can see that God is demanding the height of holiness.

If you keep the rupees you will commit only a venial sin. But we can consider this from a different angle. You could keep that one million rupees and God would be pleased, since you could do a lot of good like building hospitals, helping educational institutions, and so on. Then you might respond: "Yes, I see that and I will glorify God." Ignatius would reply: "Yes, but God would be more glorified if you gave up the money." You would probably say: "Look, do not bother me with this more-glorifying business. I am satisfied with pleasing God and doing good." Ignatius's response would be: "No retreat for you. Go home." If you had said: "If God will be more glorified by my giving up the money, then I will do so right now," you are ready for a thirty-day retreat.

There is also a third possibility. If you had said: "I don't have the strength to give up the money right now, but I wish I had the strength," I personally would give the retreat to you.

SCRIPTURE TEXTS FOR THE "FIRST PRINCIPLE AND FOUNDATION"

Luke 14:25–33: This passage speaks of leaving everything and everyone to follow Jesus, equating this to having the foresight of a person who plans a building project before beginning it, or that of a king who does not initiate a battle without determining the odds of winning. People are not ready to start the retreat if they do not have these dispositions or at least want these dispositions.

Matthew 13:44–46: Jesus speaks of working to obtain a valuable pearl. People must have this disposition for the kingdom. They must want it so much that nothing else is so precious to them as this. This passage can be combined with Matthew 19:16–30, which is the story of the rich young man who so clings to his treasure, his possessions, that he goes away sad. What is stated here is happiness, it is not gloom; Jesus did not come to spread a message of gloom. One of the catechisms says that man is created to glorify God and to enjoy him forever; enjoy him, forever, starting right now. We are created to enjoy God right now. This puts things in perspective; we are to enjoy the earth, to enjoy the world, to enjoy God, because until we enjoy God nothing else fully satisfies.

Philippians 3:3–9: Paul recounts all his assets and says: "For [Christ's] sake I have suffered the loss of all things, and I regard them as rubbish, in order that I may gain Christ." This is like the parable of the precious pearl.

Romans 8:35–39: "Who will separate us from the love of Christ?" (Rom. 8:35). Using different language, Paul mentions the very same things that Ignatius speaks of: health/sickness, honor/dishonor, riches/poverty, a long life/a short life.

I give these passages to retreatants when they are beginning the retreat, so that they start off with dispositions of great generosity, of courage, of complete surrender to God. This is exactly what Ignatius says in his "Introductory Observations," and that is probably the reason that it was only later that he incorporated the "First Principle and Foundation" into the text of the *Exercises*. In summary: the "First Principle and Foundation" gives us the outline of where Ignatius is leading the retreatants. Once the retreatants have this, they are ready to start the Exercises, and by the middle of the second week it is to be hoped that they will understand it.

2

Our Sinfulness

I will ask for a growing and intense
sorrow and tears for my sins.
— IGNATIUS LOYOLA

Becoming conscious of our sinfulness, we can recognize how
Jesus delivers us from sin. Growing in love for God involves
accepting God's immense love for us.

We can be saved only when God justifies us, makes us holy,
and unites us with himself. And the only way to all that is
through faith in him, the faith of which Paul speaks (in
Galatians 2:16 Paul shows the futility of justifying oneself
by doing works of the Mosaic Law). I have shown how an
integral part of this faith is a sense of our inadequacy, of our
worthlessness, of our sinfulness. If people do not sense the
need of being saved, salvation is pretty meaningless.

THE HUNGER FOR GOD

Today I would like to grapple a little with the concept of our
sinfulness. When I speak to non-Jesuits about an Ignatian retreat, I do not speak about the four weeks of the Spiritual

Exercises. What I do is this: I gear everything to the experience of God. Everybody's heart is hungry for an experience of God. How to attain this? The answer is threefold. I generally talk about the desire for God. When the desire is very great, one is more likely to attain this experience. Then pray: ask and you will receive. The third method that I suggest for encountering God in Christ is repentance. This is the method that Jesus was always preaching.

There are two lovely instances of this in the Book of Revelation. First, according to Revelation 3: "For you say, 'I am rich, I have prospered, and I need nothing.' You do not realize that you are wretched, pitiable, poor, blind, and naked" (Rev. 3:17). God is telling us we have never come in touch with our inadequacy, our sense of worthlessness, the sense of our wickedness, of our doing wrong. So he advises us to repent. These last are the keywords and lead to "Listen! I am standing at the door knocking . . ." Here is the opportunity. Here is the encounter. "If you hear my voice and open the door, I will come in to you" (Rev. 3:20). In view of this passage from Revelation, just what is repentance? The grace of repentance is not so much to be sorry for our sins, which is the way we have often viewed repentance. Repentance is a much deeper and much wider grace. It is the turning of the heart and the mind. We turn away from something and we turn our whole heart and mind on to God. This is repentance. Repentance would be better defined not by saying: "O my God, I am sorry for my sins," but rather by this: "O my God, I love you with all my heart and all my soul and all my strength." This is total repentance. Obviously we cannot repent if we think we already have what we are going to get through repentance. We cannot turn if we feel we are already facing what we want. That is the point.

And there is another very lovely passage in Revelation 2:5, "Remember then from what you have fallen; repent, and do the works you did at first." Once again, we fear a call to go back to our early love. This is what repentance is: Come back to our early love, not just: "I am sorry for my sins." So we find that when, in his early sermons, Jesus announces the kingdom, his message is: "Repent, for the kingdom of heaven has come near" (Matt. 3:2). Change your minds, change your hearts, and change your attitudes, because the kingdom has come.

So this is how I will divide the retreat then. In the first part, we will go in for the grace of repentance. In the second part, we will study what this kingdom is that Jesus brings. In the third part, we will reflect on accepting the joyful news. I will put all of this in the context of the New Testament.

Some time ago, I read a little book translated by a Scripture scholar named [William] Heidt, a Benedictine. Very nicely done. So I took a summary of it. For him a major theme of the Bible is to make people conscious of their sin, and then to show them that redemption is available. Or to put it another way: "God saves." And so his Son will be called Jesus, which means "Savior." He is essentially Savior, essentially salvation.

The crucial question is "What did he save us from?" The answer of the Bible is "from sin." Does Jesus save us from hunger, disease, political bondage, social injustice? Now it is a bit scandalous to answer with no. But we read "he will save his people from their sins" (Matt. 1:21). There is no announcement there that he will save his people from the domination of the Romans and from injustice. All of this comes within the context of the basic salvation that Jesus brings. "For which is easier, to say, 'Your sins are forgiven,' or to say, 'Stand up and walk'?" (Matt. 9:5). The first thing is: "Your sins are forgiven." "[F]orgive us our debts, as we also have forgiven our debtors" (Matt. 6:12). See, Jesus is quite concerned about sin. "Receive the Holy Spirit. If you forgive the sins of any, they are forgiven them; if you retain the sins of any, they are retained" (John 20:22–23). When forgiveness of sins comes, everything else follows. As long as sins are retained, so are a lot of other forms of evil! So Jesus attacks the root.

All the pain in the world comes from sin and selfishness. And if we do not tackle sin and selfishness, we just tackle symptoms. We can pass the best laws in the world, we can attack all the structures we like, but if we have not changed the hearts of people, what we have done is like taking a lunatic and tying him up. We have not cured him of his madness. The cure will come when we can change his heart. So this is what Jesus is moving toward: saving people from their sins. "[F]or this is my blood of the covenant, which is poured out for many for the forgiveness of sins" (Matt. 26:28). He is doing that, so that sin may be forgiven.

I will talk to you later on about what sin is. For the moment let me say this: We have equated sin too much with acts and deeds and laws and obligations. For Jesus sin is something much deeper. Sin is a refusal to grow, a refusal to love, a refusal to get committed, to be concerned, and to take risks. So many parables condemn the refusal to grow or to take risks. Look at the parables of the talents (Matt. 25:14–30) and the sheep and the goats (Matt. 25:32–46)— they show the refusal to be concerned. Then the parable of the tree that bears no fruit illustrates a refusal to bear fruit and to grow (Matt. 7:17–20). In that way sin is more terrifying than those little things mentioned by catechisms: for example, whether or not I said my prayers. Sin is something more radical within us. Jesus is concerned with curing this thing at the root; there is no doubt about that. A number of New Testament passages come back as Jesus' project of delivering us from sin: 1 Timothy 1:15, Hebrews 9:22, 1 John 4:10. It's as if he came here only for that: to save us from our sins (cf. Rom. 5:8–9 ["But God proves his love for us in that while we still were sinners Christ died for us. Much more surely then, now that we have been justified by his blood, will we be saved through him from the wrath of God"], and Acts 13:38–39 ["Let it be known to you therefore, my brothers, that through this man forgiveness of sins is proclaimed to you; by this Jesus everyone who believes is set free from all those sins from which you could not be freed by the law of Moses"]).

Heidt, in his translation of *A Catholic Theology of the Old Testament* by Paul Heinisch, shows that in each one of the books of the Old Testament we have exactly the same theme: God wants to render us conscious of sin. God wants to make humanity conscious of sin's horrendous effects. He wants to show humans that he is constantly ready to deliver them from sin. The same theme is repeated in the *Spiritual Exercises*. Unless we feel the need for God when we come to him in this retreat and experience our own inadequacy, we would have no need for him.

But this is only one aspect of the grace of repentance. What we have called traditionally the first week of the Exercises is really a beautiful week, not a week of rejection and gloom. We meet God in a saving context. It is the way I as a therapist would tackle a person who is a neurotic. I do not knock him or her down. I will very lovingly show them that they have to change. It is important not to go to either extreme. This is the urgency that Jesus came to communicate. The kingdom is at hand. Dance with joy, accept the joyful news. Instead, many are sad and gloomy. Think of the beatitudes in which Jesus declares how happy the people are who are poor, merciful, and peacemakers, the people who hunger and thirst for righteousness. A good retreat master can communicate the need for repentance without giving a negative feeling. People are lovely, people are beautiful—and people need to change very much.

We have to avoid the two extremes: "You are bad; there is something wrong with you. When you change I will love you." This will bring a person nowhere. Or: "You can never do wrong as far as I am concerned. Everything about you is beautiful and lovely. There is no need for you to change or grow." That is the other extreme.

The more secure the retreat master is and the more loving, the less he or she will get in the way. He or she pushes people to Scripture, so that the retreatants encounter this kind of God in their prayer and meditation. That is the whole idiom of Jesus who loves us just as we are. Look into his eyes and we can tell him all the filthiest things we want, and there he is, no change, he loves us just as we are right now. We do not have to change to get his love. When we can push people to this kind of Jesus, then they get the sense of "I am lovable."

Catholic theology has always claimed that human beings are basically good. Though we have been damaged, basically we are good. At the root of pure creation there is an act of infinite love. God falls for us; this is the unbelievable news. That means he would lose himself for us. This is too shocking, that God would be a victim of the passion that we call love. Then we are told the shocking thing that God loves us so much that he gave up his goodness for our sake! Hello! This is a bit too crazy. God went mad out of love for us. Then we must be very lovely. What we have stressed in the past is how lovely God must be that he can love us like this. But nobody has yet said how lovely we must be, that God could fall for us like this. Both are true.

Most of the people coming for a retreat have a deep sense of worthlessness; that is, they are full of not-okay feelings. Therefore I stress much more the aspect of how God loves us, *as well as* the aspect of our sinfulness. And as soon as the retreatants sense God's love, they want to change. What they need most is the realization of God's love. Most people come to us wounded today. It is not the sense of sin that they are lacking; it is the sense of lovableness. We have to communicate to people their goodness. A religious sister, for instance, might theoretically see that this is the root of her problem: She cannot praise anyone because she allows no one to praise her; she cannot love because she does not allow anyone to love her; she is giving nothing because she is not receiving anything; and she cannot see others as okay, because she will not see herself as okay. The first thing she must do is see her lovableness.

We cannot overlook sin or downplay it. I am not referring to sin in the sense of causing guilt. Seeing one's sin is being aware of one's sinfulness, as a preparation for that act of courage, which is faith in God or accepting God's love. Jesus' joyful announcement of the Good News is the message that salvation is available. In order for people to accept salvation they first of all must be made aware that they need it.

If a person is sinful—and God loves each individual just as he or she is—that is indeed thrilling news. Jesus brings this in through various Gospel accounts, such as Luke 13:1–5. Do not take that "you will all perish as they did" to mean that now we will all be whacked and punished. If we do not repent, if we do not receive the joyful news, if we do not accept the Father's Love, then we are in the same condition as all the others. Then, all of us must say: "[F]orgive us our debts, as we also have forgiven our debtors" (Matt. 6:12). We are always God's debtors. He wants us to call ourselves "worthless slaves" (Luke 17:7–10). The fact that we might have done our duty does not empower us to lay a clam upon God's graciousness; that graciousness is and always remains a gift.

Our value does not come from what we have done. Rather it comes from the Father's Love. That is where all our value comes from. That is where all our salvation comes from (1 John 4:7–12)! This is such a very forceful statement that you could put it in psychological terms. Jesus is saying: Do not be defensive. Accept the fact that you have inadequacies and fears, and that you have a lot to grow. Then you will change. Look at the parable of the Pharisee and the tax collector (Luke 18:10–14). The tax collector recognized the need of God's mercy and acknowledged his sins. The Pharisee, however, justified himself and did not acknowledge his dependence on God.

Blaise Pascal brings this out very forcefully when he comments that it is necessary to sin. In other words, he claims it is not possible that a person would not be in sin. In a similar fashion, Paul would call himself the chief of sinners (1 Tim. 1:15). In his case, he committed a sin ignorantly and because of his zeal. How very interesting! Jesus says: "They will put you out of the synagogues. Indeed, an hour is coming when those who kill you will think that by doing so they are offering worship to God. And they will do this because they have not known the Father or me" (John 16:2–3). So where is the sin in all of this? According to the definition in the catechism, we sin when we know something is wrong and we deliberately do it. People are not even aware that it is wrong; yet they do it anyway and sin! Why? Because they knowingly, and perhaps out of bad will, decided to keep themselves in ignorance with regard to what God wants. And Paul condemned himself because he persecuted the Church, even though he said he did this in good faith.

On the one hand, Jesus said: "Father, forgive them; for they know not what they do" (Luke 23:34). Why should we forgive them if they do not know what they are doing? Perhaps we should forgive them because of their ignorance or perhaps because God loves them and we should also. On the other hand, as Paul says to the Corinthians: "None of the rulers of this age understood this; for if they had, they would not have crucified the Lord of glory" (1 Cor. 2:8). And yet, what a terrible thing Jesus said: "[S]eeing they do not perceive, and hearing they do not listen, nor do they understand . . . For this people's heart has grown dull" (Matt. 13:11–17). Is a person the less guilty because of that? Of course not! He or she is still guilty. Paul says: "I am not conscious of any sin, but not for that reason am I justified." St. Augustine says that it is impossible not to sin if we do not know righteousness. In other words, precisely because we are blind and we do not know what we are doing, we are sinning. In this respect, we are doing a lot of harm.

As I said earlier, Jesus is going out of his way to show people how sinful they are. Take, for example, the parable of the talents (Matt. 25:14–30). By those standards, who would be without sin? Then read the parable of the sheep to the right and the goats at the left (Matt. 25:31–46): "I was hungry and you gave me food, I was thirsty and you gave me something to drink. . . ." By the standards of this parable, who would not be in mortal sin? We all are! Every day I am in sin. With millions hungry around me, yet I am not concerned! Apathy and sloth, in other words, sin. Untruthfulness is sin for Jesus; unproductiveness is sin. Remember the cursed fig tree in the parable (Mark 11:12–14). It is not even the season for fruit, and yet its unproductiveness signifies sin, specifically Israel's lack of readiness to accept Jesus and his message. Must one conclude that God is a terrible God? On the contrary, he is joyful news. What Jesus is saying is that we are sinful creatures. If we accept this message, we will change, provided we accept as well the Good News: God's Love.

This is a strange paradox indeed. If we take either one of the two extremes, we get superficial or we fall into a depression. If we take the extreme of our sinfulness, we fall into depression. Or we might say: "No, man, everything is grand!" That reflects superficiality; that is, no depth, no sense of the anguish of needing to be saved, of our creatureliness, of our inadequacy, of our nothingness, of the angst of life. For us it is all on the surface; life is all roses. Since we have never tasted what life is all about, we are superficial. If we put both extremes together, then we sense life in its depth and the exhilaration of being loved and redeemed. We reach the point of repentance.

Other biblical examples of this sense of repentance are to be found in the parable of the rich man and Lazarus (Luke 16:20–31); in Jesus' saying that no servant can be the slave of two masters (Luke 16:13); and in Jesus' reference to the way things were in Noah's days (Luke 17:26). The rich man and others were not condemned for any sinful action. It is just that they were so involved in the world that they had no time for God. They had lost any sense of the absolute and were all immersed in the relative.

This consciousness of sin, much like on the psychological level the awareness of one's blocks and, in some cases, of one's neuroses, is of great value. So too on the spiritual level: The awareness of one's selfishness, blocks, fears, and unproductiveness is of tremendous value, because it brings with it the exhilaration of accepting God's love, the challenge for change, and all that comes with it. Hence it is important to keep both polarities. And it is very important to communicate this to the retreatant.

If I see sin, then there is matter for rejoicing. How much evil I have done and how much I am loved! Otherwise there would be no cause for rejoicing. One of the essential graces of repentance is joy. It is the authentic, homecoming happiness. How lovely it is to surrender oneself with all one's inadequacies into the loving arms of God and be accepted. How wonderful! And this surrender is combined with tears, that is true, but not with sadness. A person feels so relieved, so close to Christ, and so happy. That is why in the *Spiritual Exercises* Ignatius called these "tears that move to the love of God" (no. 316). The motivation may come from one's sins, from the Passion of Christ, or from the Trinity. When a person actually experiences repentance, everything falls into place. When one only looks at the text of Ignatius, it seems like a negative, festering, not-okay feeling. But these tears are encouraged only to intensify the sense of our acceptance, and the sense of how much God loves us and how really good we are. It is indeed a paradox. This experience is similar to an alcoholic saying to his wife: "Wasn't it wonderful I went through that period of alcoholism, because nothing would have brought out your love for me as much as that?"

Sin has its purpose: to bring out the love of God! Sin is neither an unmitigated evil nor an obstacle to the grace of God, his love, and his mercy. That is why St. Paul says, "where sin increased, grace abounded all the more" (Rom. 5:20). Sin is an evil; so we must abjure sin. To have sinned is a value to be treasured; that is, when it is followed by repentance. It is better to have sinned than not to have sinned. But do not sin on that account. When the retreatant can see sin in that light, there comes so much joy into his or her heart, because there is no place for useless regrets, such as "I wasted my life," etc. The sinner can forgive himself or herself. You have sinned: Congratulations! How much will you get out of that experience now? That is the point of many of the parables. Take, for example, the parable of the Prodigal Son (Luke 15:11–32). The lucky fellow, he sinned and he got more. Or look at the case of the lost sheep (Luke 15:4–7). Now there is a great mystery. To have sinned has deep value.

God breaks through a person's ignorance not through revelation but through love. And that is why revelation is not so much talk as deed. God saves, heals, loves, and becomes one of us: This is true revelation. Then we can let go and see ourselves in our ugliness, knowing that God loves us.

Although good can come from sin, we cannot deny the seriousness of sin. I suspect that talk about hell is a mythological way of showing the seriousness of sin. What a horrible thing sin is! It impedes love, life, growth, and union with God. Unfortunately, we have begun to take that mythological thing quite literally. So, when I give a retreat, I get off the topic of punishment. I want to do something much more basic; namely, I want to show how much we need God, how ignorant we are, and how immensely God loves us!

One retreatant lately experienced the problem of wanting to be accepted by everyone. He thought that as a true disciple he had to love everybody. The problem is that his ideal was up in the clouds and his ignorance was that he thought he was right up there already. The mistake is thinking that one can do this right now; a human person cannot. And when people realize this, they can relax and really start moving toward their ideal. But if a person takes that ideal and puts it onto themselves now, then he or she is acting out a phony thing. If, however, a person says, "I see the ideal, but I am not there yet," then I would respond: "I don't like this particular person, but I am infatuated with another person." Or: "Toward you I feel warm, but I don't really care for you," etc. This is honest. Then we are aware of our weakness and likely to grow.

So, then, what does our Lord mean when he asks us to love everyone as he loves us? We have to remember that he also said: "Be perfect as your heavenly Father is perfect." That should be our guiding star. Most religious formation programs are geared to do just this. All of us religious are uneasy about the fact that our novices are not as perfect as they should be. So we try to hasten the process to make sure they will get it within one year. The result is that we communicate a different message: Put on an act and prove that you have got it.

In the past, people used to stress that love was in the will, not in the feelings. Although this is still true, I would phrase it differently: "My will is to love everyone. I really want to love everyone. However, my actual state is that I do not love everyone. So now I want to learn how to love more people. Nevertheless, the basic will is there, because I could also make a decision that I do not want to come close to others. That would be a sin."

In order to love others we have to love ourselves. Yet in order to be able to love ourselves, we have to be loved by at least one person. Now, a very few lucky people get this from God. For some people's psychological well-being this might not be needed. However, if one's spiritual sense is deep and he or she has gone deeper into life, then it is vital. Without it, sooner or later we start to gripe and believe that life is meaningless. It is then that we sense that this emptiness is itself full; that darkness is light. Having this acceptance from God, a person might still be psychologically a neurotic; sometimes, however, this realization overflows into the emotional, and then it is beautiful.

Some people feel like blaming God about this sin business, since we cannot help but sin.

Such people would do well to read a passage from St. Paul's Epistle to the Romans: "Nor is that all; something similar happened to Rebecca when she had conceived children by one husband, our ancestor Isaac. Even before they had been born or had done anything good or bad (so that God's purpose of election might continue, not by works but by his call) she was told, 'The elder shall serve the younger.' As it is written, 'I have loved Jacob, but I have hated Esau'" (Rom. 9:10–13). There one will find: divine life, sin, retribution, stubbornness of heart, mercy, forces of evil, and forces of good. Or look to Origen [c. 185–254], one of the greatest of all Christian theologians, who said that in the end all will be saved, and the official Church condemned him.

One might then complain that sin is just a trick to better show God's love. Here we must remember that we are just silly creatures, speaking from our silly reason. If we come with reason, of course we will find contradictions everywhere. St. Paul is great in those chapters of Romans. He does not explain anything; he does not solve [through reason] any of the problems he states there. However, the reader knows that he has solved them in his heart. An example of this would be Romans 5:21, where Paul says that "just as sin exercised dominion in death, so grace might also exercise dominion through justification leading to eternal life through Jesus Christ our Lord."

Without sin we would not feel the ecstasy, the agony, of God's love. Why has God chosen this way? God alone knows. If we feel like swearing at him, then let's go ahead and swear; let's get it off our chest. And we will see things a bit better perhaps. Remember, however, that this realization is not accomplished through speculation, but through contemplation.

THE SOCIAL DIMENSION OF SIN

In order to get an idea of sin and even a hatred for sin, I think the modern retreatant is best helped by becoming aware of the social dimensions of sin. This is put very well in one of the stories from *Prayers* by Michel Quoist, where he describes walking through a hospital, from one pavilion of suffering to another. He then cries out in anguish, "Why, Lord, why this suffering?" And he got the answer: "It is not

I who caused this. It is you who did it." Suffering is a consequence of sin. Indeed, all sin brings suffering with it.

We often ask, "How can we understand sin existentially?" Stand before Christ on the Cross and do so today! I remember one priest in Bombay who was paralyzed for years. I stood before him asking myself, "Did I do this?" Maybe I did! If it is true that we are all one body, and if it is true that sin always brings disorder and suffering, then I possibly caused his suffering as much as I caused the suffering of Christ. The Jews, as well as the Hindus, have a tradition that if someone is suffering then they have sinned. Catholic theology does not accept this. On the other hand, Catholic theology does accept that if a person is suffering it is because of sin, even somebody else's sin. In this light, then, if I have sinned, I take responsibility for the suffering in the world.

Gandhi was a great believer in this, and it got him into political trouble. When there was the earthquake in Bihar, he said it was the result of sin. People got very angry with him because of this statement. There are dimensions, vibrations, and areas of reality of which we know very little. How do spiritual disorder, selfishness, and hate vibrations affect material reality and affect health? Do selfishness, hate, and pride have physical repercussions? Are these emotional or psychological?

I remember reading in Swami Ramdas something related. Some of you have heard this before, but I think it's important for you to hear it again. Somebody said to him: "There is an atheist in Europe who remarked, 'If I ever would meet that God who causes so much suffering, I would strangle him.'" And Ramdas replied, "If I met this man, I would take his hands very gently and put them at his own throat and say, 'Go ahead, strangle him. Here is the cause of all the suffering.

If you have sinned, you have caused all the suffering. Take responsibility for that.'"

When there was still more turmoil in the Church, I used to ask the retreatants, "Who is responsible, the liberals or the conservatives?" No, all our sin is the cause. It is easy to blame the bishops and others. If there is harm done, it is through sin. My presence in the Church may be harming the Church; my presence in the community may also be harmful. In contrast, when I am grace-filled, my presence in the community affects the whole community. Pierre Teilhard de Chardin brought it out very powerfully when he said, "Strike a bronze gong in one place, and the whole gong reverberates." You cannot strike one member of the community without the whole community reverberating. The whole Church reverberates.

Applying this to the apostolate would mean striving with all our might to eradicate sin. Jesus sees the healing of the natural order in terms of the forgiveness of sin. James 5:14 says exactly the same. "Are any among you sick? They should call for the elders of the church and have them pray over them, anointing them with oil in the name of the Lord."

To eradicate sin, to turn people away from their selfishness, is the most important social work we can do. When we are tackling ignorance, disease, poverty, and unjust structures, we are tackling the symptoms, not the root cause. Unless we grapple with the root of selfishness and sin, what is the use? It is like treating a cancer patient with aspirin. Or we take a man who is mad and we lock him up. In doing so, we have not cured him. Neither does legislation solve all our problems. In fact, it is, in a way, despairing. So how do we truly handle this thing?

Jesus certainly did approach suffering that way. We need

to tackle the big devil. Not hunger and unemployment—these are small devils, no doubt—but the root of it all is sin and selfishness. So the calamity is not that so many people are starving, and through legislation we will force people to give them money. The terrible calamity is that we, as their brothers and sisters, have to be forced to give help. This will breed other evils, sooner or later. Still, nobody has tackled the fact that we have to be forced to do it.

Most retreatants respond to this and get their sense of sinfulness from their sense of responsibility to the human race. If I commit an act of selfishness in my room, the whole of humanity is involved. Every act is a turning point in history. Every act changes perspectives everywhere. Again, this observation should not come from a point of view of breeding fear.

3

Repentance

What have I done for Christ? What am I doing for Christ? What ought I to do for Christ?
— IGNATIUS LOYOLA

Repentance brings an intense desire for God, deep gratitude, and a growth in self-awareness that increases our freedom to love.

In this section I will put my remarks about the first week of the Spiritual Exercises under three headings: fruit of the first week; the examination of conscience; and the method and dangers of the first week.

THE FRUIT OF THE FIRST WEEK

During the first week one danger the retreat master must be aware of is the tendency to push the retreatant into sadness, discouragement, or self-hatred. The consideration of sin tends to lead people to this conclusion quite easily.

What are the fruits of the first week then? One of them is sorrow for sin, which is not the same as sadness ([I should desire] "a growing and intense sorrow and tears for my sins," no. 55). This sorrow contains joy and peace. Anybody who has experienced this will feel a great relief and peace. *Felix culpa!* Oh happy fault! How fortunate that we sinned! Blessed Peter Faber (1506–1546) has been quoted somewhere as saying: "Even if the Holy Spirit scolds, he scolds you so gently, so sweetly."

Another fruit is the gift of tears. This fruit represents a move toward the love of God. Tears form one of the gifts of which Ignatius speaks. The retreatant cannot produce them. He or she has to ask and desire this fruit and even do penance for it. Tears are a precious grace of that first week. This can be noticed in other schools of mysticism also. The Zen masters give great importance to tears; the false ego is washed away through them.

Another fruit of the first week is the intense desire for God. This desire is the foundation of everything else. Indeed it is part of repentance. Without a very great desire for God one gets nothing out of the long retreat or any retreat. Take, for example, the following illustration. A man goes to the sadhu every day and says he wants to experience God. The sadhu gives no reply and the man comes back again and again and again. After many days the sadhu says: "This man seems to be an earnest seeker of God." So he tells him: "When I go down for a bath to the river, come and meet me there." Then both enter the water and the sadhu pushes the man's head under the water for a minute or two. He is struggling to get out. When the sadhu releases him, he says: "Come to me under the banyan tree. When I held your head under the water, you were struggling to get out. Why?" "Because I was gasping for air." The sadhu told him: "The day you desire God so earnestly as you desired air when you were under the water, that day you will find him."

So if one has not yet found God, he or she does not really desire God. This is very true. We desire too many other things besides God. We have got our worries, distractions, and so forth. Even in the lives of most saints, where the "one-pointedness" sets in, then they want nothing but God, and they make the breakthrough. That was the way with most of our Indian saints. Tukaram [an Indian poet and saint (1577–1650) in the Hindu tradition] went to the jungle and said: "I won't eat nor sleep until he appears to me; he has to!"

These penances and vigils: It is all or nothing! I have got to find God. Once I met a Japanese monk and asked him how he made the breakthrough to enlightenment. He said he entered a monastery at the age of seventeen, and one of the things he did was prostrations, constant prostrations in search of the Absolute. He did not sleep in a bed for three months. He would sit in a chair, doze off, and then rise up again in prostrations. He was determined either to die or to make a breakthrough. These are dangerous techniques, and I do not tell people to go in for the show, but for the spirit behind them.

Another fruit is the experience of one's sinfulness together with God's loving kindness. As a matter of fact, the second comes first. First, people experience God's loving kindness; then they can relax enough to experience their own sinfulness and ugliness. The full experience of our sinfulness would not be possible without experiencing the loving kindness of God. William Barclay somewhere points out the progression in the spiritual life of Saint Paul, whose first experience of God's love occurs when he encounters the risen Christ on the road to Damascus. Later Paul calls himself first "an apostle . . . through Jesus Christ" (Gal. 1:1), but says: "For I am the least of the apostles, unfit to be called an apostle, because I persecuted the church of God" (1 Cor. 15:9). Then in Ephesians we find: "I am the very least of all the saints" (Eph. 3:8); and finally in 1 Timothy 1:15 we read that "Christ Jesus came into the world to save sinners—of whom I am the foremost." What a contrast from the young Paul who persecuted Christians in the name of the Law.

There is a nice prayer of St. Anselm (c. 1033–1109) that brings out beautifully that we have first to experience the love of God and then repentance will follow: "O Lord, our God, give us the grace to desire you with our whole heart, so that desiring you we may seek and find you, and finding you we may love you, and loving you we may hate those things which have separated us from you." We generally think that first we have to hate our sins, but we do not even know what our sin is until we come into the light, as it was with Paul who was blinded by Christ's radiance. The sense of sin follows the encounter with Christ.

We have many instances in the New Testament of this. As we've talked about already, first Paul meets Christ, and then he realizes that what he thought was virtue was really sin. Other examples are Zacchaeus, the reformed tax collector (Luke 19:1–10); the woman who was a sinner (Luke 7:36–50); and Isaiah, who admitted his "unclean lips" (Isa. 6:1–13).

Ignatius had deep experiences of the discernment of spirits, another example of God's love; and only then did he become aware of his sinfulness. All the prayers and colloquies of the first week bring this out. The point behind all this can be seen in the following: "I will conclude with a colloquy, extolling the mercy of God our Lord, pouring out my thoughts to him, and giving thanks to him that up to this very moment he has granted me life. I will resolve with his grace to amend for the future" (no. 61). There is a loving presence behind everything, sustaining me and loving me, protecting me and shielding me. Ignatius wants the retreatant to get this: how tender and loving God is toward me!

Then we encounter the fruit of total generosity. "What shall I do for Christ?" It is upon the answer to that question that the retreat master judges whether a person is ready for the second week or not. Finally, intense gratitude is another fruit. This would include all aspects of the total grace of repentance: the joy, the love, the gratitude, the sorrow for sin, and the rejoicing in the face of the fact that we have sinned. Repent and believe the joyful news!

THE EXAMINATION OF CONSCIENCE

When I used to give this talk to people, say, eight or nine years ago, they would not even want to hear the words *examination of conscience*. It was as if they were dirty words; one needs only to love people, forget about oneself, and move out to others. The belief was "The less you think of yourself the better. The more you think of loving others, the better for everybody concerned." Prayer, penance, and everything like that used to turn people off. Then I came to realize that it was really a matter of semantics. I would get them to fast for two or three days, but I never called it penance! I had to call it the development of inner consciousness or something similar.

A well-known retreat preacher, an American, once told us that a famous psychiatrist gave some seminar on recent discoveries that were tremendous and gave very rich re-

sults. Only twelve people were allowed to attend the seminar and they paid heavy fees. Anyhow, two Jesuits managed
to get in. The psychiatrist called it the regulation of self-
motivated something-or-other. It turned out to be nothing
less than a seminar on the "Daily Particular Examination of
Conscience"! Everybody was thrilled about it. But if it had
been called the "Particular Examen," it would have been
thrown out the window.

There is a point to examination: finding out what needs
improvement. Every institution, in order to prevent itself
from fossilization, needs to have a built-in challenge to itself,
usually a small group of people who serve as its conscience. It
is fatal for the institution if it stifles that conscience, either
from lethargy or triumphalism. Similarly, this is one of the
wise points of a good superior. I believe [Pedro] Arrupe had
this. He said: "Don't throw the radicals out. You need them.
They will make mistakes, they will get you into all kinds of
troubles, they are very uncomfortable to have around, some
of them are obviously wrong and some of them are clearly
right. But at the moment you don't know who is right and
who is wrong, you can find out only in perspective. But we
need them, they have to be inside the body because this
keeps us alive."

At one point Arrupe said he was learning more and more
the wisdom of the Lord's saying about the wheat and the
weeds [Matt. 13:24–30]. Wait, be patient until you can distinguish the good from the bad. So we need to be constantly
challenged. Sometimes certain people among us serve as this
challenge.

The instance in which I really discovered the value of the
examination of conscience was when we had to bring our
taped interview to the counseling classes. There for the first

time I realized that I was saying things of which I was not aware, asking questions of which I was not aware, giving in to feelings of which I was not aware. That is why I consider it a great help to listen to one's own tapes from a therapy session, not only when one is being counseled, but also as counselor. We learn a lot about ourselves and the counselee and can sharpen our skills. In fact, what we are doing then is self-examination. Otherwise what we are really doing is shooting birds while in flight. The same holds true in our everyday life. So much is lost simply because we do not sit back and take stock. So that is one idea of the value of the examination of conscience.

The second notion is that the price of freedom is eternal vigilance. If people want to be free, they have to be eternally vigilant. One of the great commentators on the *Spiritual Exercises*, [Ignacio] Casanovas, said: "A house which contains treasures, if not guarded, will soon lose those treasures." We must constantly watch who is coming in and who is going out, lest we lose them. To prove that freedom needs awareness and vigilance, take the example of a hypnotized man. During hypnosis he is commanded to bring a certain book from the library to a certain man the next day. He will do so the next day, not knowing why. He is not aware of that which is impelling him, and therefore he is not free. When people are aware of what is impelling them, they can then act freely. If they are not even aware, they are under compulsion.

Let me give another example. In the old days I would lose pencils and pens galore. I was not even aware where I had put them. Now the more a person does this sort of thing, the more unfree are his or her actions; they are automatic, not free. Imagine such a person meeting people, talking to them, directing them, and not even being aware of what he or she is saying or what is really going on. There is no freedom in that. People are only free if they are aware of what they are doing.

A Spanish philosopher wrote a lovely essay in which he speaks about freedom through awareness. He says that most of us are sensed billiard balls on a pool table. We are pushed around. People have sensations, but billiard balls do not. That is about all the difference there is, not much more. People's background, their history, their environment—these all push them in different directions and they feel they have no con.... The first step in getting control so as not to be pushed a... ...nd is to become aware. Oh, the painstaking process of ....ning home, of being aware of what is going on! W...... are these drives coming from? Who is pushing me? There is no substitute for this awareness, this coming home to oneself. See how superficial it is to say: "Forget yourself and lose yourself in others." Indeed, this is extremely superficial. In fact, the tragedy is that if people are not aware of what is going on in themselves, they are doing harm to others; not losing themselves to others, but doing positive harm to the people they want to help. In doing counseling we must be aware of both roles, that of the participant and that of the observer. One must participate by watching the client and watching oneself. Unless the counselors do this, they will lose themselves in their clients and will not even be aware of what they are doing to them.

In regard to inner freedom, I would suggest the following exercise. Sit down in one place, stop reading, turn the radio off, and so on. Ask yourself, "Where is my freedom?"

Freedom is the ability to do what one wants to do. It is like when you want to walk to the dining room, but one leg wants to go to one side, one to the other, the head is turned in the wrong direction, and so forth. If that is what is happening inside us, then we cannot do what we want. Total chaos pulls in all directions: a perfect picture of what is going on inside us. What kind of freedom is this? Rather we must look toward the freedom to love. People have no freedom to love until they are really aware of themselves.

Here is an idea that I picked up once from a book by a psychiatrist. He said: "Some temperaments would rather search for the Holy Grail than slay the dragon." In the twentieth century, we are Grail hunters rather than dragon killers. We would stress love of neighbor rather than hatred of self, the Incarnation rather than the Crucifixion. Our century is appalled by the previous centuries; people of previous centuries were obsessed with self and with flight. They seemed to lack love and closeness. They would have been appalled to think that we would attempt the love of God without the uprooting of inordinate attachments or attempting to find the Grail without slaying the dragon. Aldous Huxley said, "Our kingdom go" is a necessary corollary of "Thy Kingdom come." It really boils down to this: Self-awareness is essential for love, yet the matter of losing oneself in love can be very misleading.

Ignatius gives us a type of method to help. The examination of conscience is a very delightful exercise. We discover so much. We learn so much. It is a kind of exercise in self-awareness, if people do not take it as a kind of exercise in self-hatred or self-criticism in the negative sense (which is how it was unfortunately presented in the past). It is not even necessarily a means for self-improvement, as if one might say, "I'll notice my defects, and I will correct my defects." This can be fatal. It is like one side of me going against the other side: the child misbehaves and the parent comes and corrects. This is similar to the critical parent spanking the child. That is bad indeed, and then the whole exercise becomes distasteful. If people make an exercise in awareness, where they are aware of the different events of the day, where they relive them, then they will get in touch with their feelings. In this there is no self-condemnation. Just look, just observe, and things begin to change. Notice a kind of a depth coming into our lives. And even the exercise itself is quite delightful, in a very subtle way, very profitable and delightful. Ignatius makes a whole method of prayer out of this. He begins by telling us to thank God for all the graces, ask for light, review the day, and then he recommends an act of contrition and a purpose of amendment.

Now, I would adapt that a bit. Begin by praising and thanking God. Praise always uplifts the heart. The secret is to always be joyful and to be forever thankful. People should thank God for something specific that they find in the day and for which they want particularly to thank him. I find this is a great help. Because when a person says: "Thank God for graces," the whole thing is so general. "What is the one thing I want to thank God for today?" That makes it much easier. A person could spend a minute or two on that. What particular graces have I received today? People can say to themselves, "If I haven't received any grace today, then I was not at home." This is because God is sending deliveries constantly.

A Jesuit mystic said somewhere: "If we could get even a faint glimpse of the number of graces God is giving us at every minute, we would think those graces are reserved for saints like Francis Xavier." God is lavish! But a person has to be at home to receive God's graces. In order to establish contact with God, one must establish contact with one's own self. If people are a stranger to themselves, how can they be close to God? They will obviously be strangers to God and strangers to others. Then, going over the day, if a person is particularly distracted, it helps to write down the events of the day. First event, second event . . . Sometimes one or two are enough. We do not have to make this a complete exercise. Just two or three events are sufficient. In other words, "What was the best thing I did today? What was the worst?" That is enough. There is a lot of material there. A third way of reviewing the events of the day would be to ask oneself: "Have I been fervent today? If so, why? If not, why not?"

Ignatius gives enormous importance to this examination of conscience. So much importance did he give to it that he would dispense people from meditation and praying the breviary quite easily (because of sickness, headache, or tiredness). But Ignatius never dispensed them from the examination of conscience. We must always keep that as part of our striving for self-awareness.

In short, the unreflected life is not worthy of reflection. So, if people are really going to live, they need that kind of reflection. We have to turn in on ourselves and be aware of ourselves. Even to the scholastics, Ignatius gave only one hour of prayer and, out of this, they were supposed to do half an hour of examination. The reason that he gave it so much importance was that he took it as a means for the discernment of spirits. What spirits are moving me?

As I have said earlier, when there is no movement in the

retreatant, he has lapsed into tepidity. This can in due measure be applied to life. A person comes to his or her examination of conscience and asks: "What is the state I am in now? Consolation, desolation, fervor, lack of fervor, aridity, dryness, or what? Spiritually, where am I?" And the retreatant answers, "Nothing, neutral." Hear the alarm signal: neither consolation nor desolation; this is an alarm signal! A different approach might be, "What spirit was guiding me today? What decision did I take today?"

One final general remark that I borrowed from [Ignacio] Casanovas: The purpose of the examination is to increase our love. It is not to come away discouraged. If a person has fire and pours water on it, it will go out. But if one adds gasoline, it blazes. The idea is to make the examination so that when people pour all their defects, shortcomings, and the rest into it, the fire will burn even more brightly. Do not dampen or quench the fire. The examination of conscience is a repetition of the first week of the Exercises. One does not end up discouraged, but rather asks, "What have I done for Christ? What am I doing for Christ?" People feel the love of God so much during a period of examination that they go away eager to do great things for Christ. This can be done only if they review their day under the gaze of Christ; and that gaze is a loving gaze. He is looking at us with great love. This really does something to people when they come before Christ and he looks at them. One might reflect, "Another day wasted. Lots of defects. I did the things I didn't want to do. I spoiled everything." But then he or she looks into the eyes of Christ, and what has happened makes no difference whatsoever. He loves each one just as much.

THE METHOD AND DANGERS OF THE FIRST WEEK

What is the method of prayer in the first week? How do you get the fruit? Follow this principle attributed to Ignatius: "Do everything as if everything depends on you, and pray as if everything depends on God." The idea is that we do all we can to get the fruit, and at the same time realize that all is pure grace. The fruit is attained through God's love and not through effort. So I recommend the use of the Psalms, ejaculatory prayers, and petitions. In addition, the Benedictine method of prayer, *lectio divina*, is very good. It involves reading a Psalm or other Scripture passage and going over it repeatedly. This is more likely to produce fruit than mere discursive prayer. Still another method is that of colloquies and petitions. See what Ignatius says in no. 53 regarding how a colloquy is made, as one friend speaks to his friend. This grace is attained by talking with Christ. Here imaginative faith is quite helpful, especially through repetitions, which approach the prayer of simplicity. St. Alphonsus Liguori (1696–1787) defines the *prayer of simplicity* as follows: "At the end of a certain time, ordinary meditation produces what is called acquired contemplation, which consists in seeing at a simple glance the truths which could previously be discovered only through prolonged discourse." And finally, simply use silent prayer. If you can stay in complete silence, spend all the time in that. The fruit will be given to the retreatant; repentance will come. Perhaps a person may experience it in a flash at some other time during the day.

I offer retreatants a few Scripture passages to use in their meditations. There are dozens from which to choose. I generally give selections such as Luke 7: 37–39, the woman who was a sinner, who bathed Christ's feet with her tears and dried them with her hair. I love to give them those texts that have graces like love, gratitude, and sorrow for sin in the encounter with Christ. Then Acts 9:1–22, the conversion of Paul; Luke 15:3–32, those three parables: the lost sheep, the lost coin, the lost son; Luke 19:1–10, on Zacchaeus. I sometimes recommend that the retreatants make an Ignatian contemplation on all these things, reliving the scene, and so forth.

Another couple of selections are 1 Timothy 1:15 and John 21:15–19. When Jesus confronts Peter after his sin, he asks only: "Do you love me?" That is one thing I insist on with the retreatants. Sin is forgiven through love. "Yes, Lord, you know that I love you." The way for sins to be forgiven is to love much and to forgive everyone else. All that other stuff about confessing every detail is very secondary. Simply love Jesus and forgive everyone. Then take those passages from Revelation 2:1–7 and 3:14–22.

Allow me to say a word about the dangers of the first week. Spiritual dangers are false guilt; refusal to forgive oneself; the desire to have a clean slate. A false sense of unworthiness is rather common among retreatants. I often say to people that sin is no obstacle to God's grace: God can always reach us. However, a real obstacle to grace is a sense of unworthiness. No matter what their sins—the sky is the limit—all people could have the experience of Paul's seventh heaven right now, today. Do they usually expect that? Not at all. After all the sins people have confessed, they have tremendous expectations, but they do not receive tremendously. They block themselves: That is the obstacle. Yet sin itself is not an obstacle at all.

Another spiritual danger is that of experiencing God as

a demand rather than a gift. He is always demanding, asking more, a kind of a killjoy. It is that kind of attitude, a fear, that warns, "Watch out when you receive Christ, the Spirit." What demands will he make? Previously people experienced Christ as a gift when they realized all he had done for them, to be thrilled by and enjoyed; now they experience him as a demand, someone who always wants them to do more. And that is why I say to people, "Never give in to the demands of Christ. Give in to the demands of your own love for him, because if you give in to his demands when you don't have so much love; you will resent him." God loves a cheerful giver! And if people do not give cheerfully, they will end up resentful. They should end up saying: "Sorry, Lord, you want that? Increase the love in my heart so that I may give it joyfully. For the time being I am saying no. I would like to give it, but make me love you more. Increase my love. Give me your love and your grace. This is enough for me."

Asking for his love and grace means asking him to give you his divine consolation. That has now been proven exegetically by commentators on the Exercises. What Ignatius is asking Christ to do is to "flood my heart with your divine consolations," meaning that I ask that "my heart [be] inflamed with the love for you [Christ] so that I can love nothing else on the face of the earth. Give me that, and then take the Lord and receive." "So you want all this?" "Give me something," or as St. Augustine would say, "Give me what you ask and then ask for whatever you want. Then I can give it joyfully, without fear, resentment, or guilt." So do not be overeager to give God things. People must not give in to the demands of the lover, but to the demands of their love. Then they can see this in human relations also. This then is one of the dangers of the first week: "What am I going to do for Christ? On my part, everything in the world!" So, watch out! Some might say, "I am still weak; but I will do it all the same!" Ask for strength instead, but do not push.

The final danger is the desire to placate God. Such an approach shows no sense of his unconditional love. Penance, springing from a desire to placate an angry God, would hamper one's relationship with Christ.

Some of the methods I have used to forestall these dangers are like the method of a Protestant pastor: Jesus Christ is present here; he loves me just as I am; so make an exercise of that, taking in the unconditional love of Christ. Another method is that of St. Teresa: Look at him looking at you, so lovingly, so humbly. Then there is the Jesus Prayer, where I invent names for Jesus and where Jesus invents names for me. Even in that colloquy we ask ourselves: "What have I done for Christ? What am I doing for Christ?" I tell the retreatant: "What great work could you do for Christ? The greatest work you can do for him is to believe in his love." See John 6:29: "This is the work of God, that you believe in him whom he has sent."

There are tremendous echoes of St. Paul here. The work is having the courage to trust. God is communicating to the retreatant, "Believe in me; believe in my love for you." Such an experience brings a great sense of liberation. Another approach is the essence of the devotion to the Sacred Heart. Though I would demythologize a lot of what St. Margaret Mary Alacoque (1647–1690) says, I believe that there is a deep spiritual message behind all those visions. And I do believe in some of the promises, such as that all those who practice this devotion will experience in their spiritual life a progress beyond their wildest expectation. And all those who propagate it will experience in the apostolate a progress beyond their wildest expectation. The whole substance of this is accepting Jesus Christ as the Incarnation of the Father's Love. Christ is Love. Christ is unconditional Love. People need to accept that. Then, of course, their whole spiritual life will flower. And if we could get people to accept this, what a transformation that would be!

4

The Kingdom of Christ

*Consider what the answer of good subjects ought to be
to a king so generous and noble-minded.*
— IGNATIUS LOYOLA

*Turning our minds and hearts totally to Christ means taking
up our cross, following him, and recognizing meaning in
pain. By living with Christ through the use of our
imagination, we can fall in love with him and his way of
life.*

Jesus begins his public life with the words "Repent, and believe the gospel" (Mark 1:15). In other words, Jesus calls us
to turn our hearts and minds totally to God. The goal of the
first week of the Spiritual Exercises is a complete change of
heart and mind; a turn in our values, our morality, our love,
our desires, and our basic orientation. "What shall I do for
Christ?" As we begin the second week of the Exercises, the
answer ought to be that we should believe the joyful news
since the kingdom of God is at hand (cf. Mark 1:16). So
there is a kingdom and a king! "He will be great, and will be
called the Son of the Most High, and the Lord God will
give to him the throne of his ancestor David. He will reign
over the house of Jacob forever" (Luke 1:32–33). Jesus is

clearly given the title of king. The idea of the kingdom is not so fanciful after all: "of his kingdom there will be no end" (Luke 1:33).

THE KINGDOM OF CHRIST

More often than not when we search in the Gospels for this kingship of Christ, we find instead a preacher, a wonder-worker, a healer, a friend of sinners. Hardly ever a king. Some Scripture scholars will equate *messiah* with *king*. We see Jesus renouncing this. When they want to make him king, he gets out of it. So where is this king of which the angel spoke?

During Christ's Passion we see him in the praetorium saying, "Yes, I am king." Here it is, out in the open . . . but "My kingdom is not from this world" (John 18:36). It is quite interesting where Christ comes out quite openly as king: Jesus on the cross (king of the Jews), Jesus before Pilate, and Jesus in the praetorium where the soldiers genuflect, slap him, spit on him, and say, "Hail, king!" This is truly a masterpiece where Jesus is now taking on the title of a king and laughing at the whole world. If all the mystics that ever lived had put their heads together, they could not have put it better than in that drama, where we have the purple robe, the crown, and all this.

Here I sometimes ask the retreatant to make a contemplation. Kneel before Jesus. Christ does not say a word yet his whole person speaks. We hear those haunting words of Luke 24:26: "Was it not necessary that the Messiah should suffer these things and then enter into his glory?" Soon the message begins filtering through. This is what he had tried to teach his disciples all along. *It was necessary.* And then we have Matthew 16:17 ("Blessed are you, Simon son of Jonah! For flesh and blood has not revealed this to you, but my Father in heaven"), and Matthew 16:21–23, where Jesus brings this message out so powerfully. Now somebody has got the secret that Jesus had guarded as his own till now. He waited until the Father would reveal it. Now he revealed it to Peter. Peter had said: "You are the Messiah, the Son of the living God." And Jesus responded, "Blessed are you."

John is filled with the same message (John 14–17). If there is one thing that emerges clearly from the Gospels, it is that the kingdom goes together with persecution. The kingdom is accompanied by opposition and contradiction. We would like to think that Jesus came to bring union of hearts. He did exactly the opposite. He said, "I have not come to bring peace, but a sword. For I have come to set a man against his father, and a daughter against her mother . . . and one's foes will be members of one's own household" (Matt. 10:34–36). Even when Jesus was a little baby, Simeon was predicting this (Luke 2:34). He will be a stumbling block. From the point of view of the apostolate, I often ask, "How come we are not stumbling blocks? How come we are not persecuted?" We have stopped preaching the Gospel; we are preaching dogma and all those things. Ignatius prayed every day that the Society would always be persecuted.

Here I would suggest a sort of colloquy. Why all this? Jesus always told his disciples that to suffer and to die is necessary. But he never said a single word to explain why. No reason at all! So we look at him silently and put away the logic of reason and put on the logic of faith and of the heart. And we accept him on his own terms: "Lord, I am ready to go with you to prison and to death." But being weak like Peter, I will ask for three graces, as in the Spiritual Exercises: "poverty as opposed to riches"; "insults or contempt as opposed to the honor of this world"; "humility as opposed to pride"—nos. 146 and 147.

First, ask for the grace of not being deaf to his call. [Dietrich] Bonhoeffer (1906–1945) says that when Christ calls a person, he bids him come and die. So do not be fooled when he says, "Come and die." At this point we cannot exercise selective hearing. He makes it plain. Luke 14:25–33 brings that out very well. Jesus discourages the people who want to follow him. Jesus said that they should renounce everything; otherwise they can't be his disciples. I do not get the impression that Jesus wanted large crowds to follow him.

Second, ask for the grace of understanding—to think as God thinks, not as humans think. What an extremely difficult task: God's view, not ours. This we cannot get except through revelation, except through grace. The heavenly Father has to give this to us. This can be found very much in Paul. He is full of this understanding. First Corinthians 1–3 shows the folly-wisdom of God's people, that if anyone wants to become wise, he should become a fool. This is a kind of wisdom we cannot get when we are worldly, and nobody can give this to us. No retreat master can explain it. In Matthew 11:25 Jesus says, "I thank you, Father, Lord of heaven and earth, because you have hidden these things from the wise and the intelligent and have revealed them to infants." If we want to understand this, we have to become a little child, and God will stoop down and make us his confidant. St. Thomas Aquinas used to say when people asked him where he got his wisdom: "I go to pray, and become like a little child, and then God tells me everything." The apostles themselves did not understand this, *even after* the Resurrection. Only when the Holy Spirit came did they begin to understand. This kind of thing we do not get in a class of theology. We could read all the works of Karl Rahner (1904–1984) and we still would not understand it.

Third, to ask for the grace to follow Christ all your life. Paul is left bewildered by his experience on the Damascus road. Light from the Lord comes through Ananias: "I myself will show him how much he must suffer for the sake of my name" (Acts 9:16). An antiphon goes: "We adore you, O Christ, and we bless you, because by your Holy Cross you have redeemed the world" (an antiphon used for the Stations of the Cross). How do we adore Christ? By being obedient unto death, death on a cross, and sharing in his suffering (cf. Phil. 3:10). Paul was one of the most joyous of the saints. We must keep that in mind too. He was very human, depressed, up and down, concerned, yet full of joy and optimism. The Gospel is not a gospel of gloom! This is the mystery. Christ has said: "Believe the joyful news" (Mark 1:15), and "How blessed are the poor" (Luke 6:20). This is the happiness that we experience right now, not in heaven, but today. The happy fool carries his cross and dances.

To follow Christ literally in the spirit of the Gospel means doing so in hardships. In poverty, for sure. Christian suffering follows when one lives and preaches the Gospel. Then the followers of Christ are bound to have hardships, poverty, opposition, and persecution. One cannot live in comfort and spread the Gospel. One cannot live the Gospel and be rich, because there are so many poor people around. The Gospel means hardship and poverty. It means being considered a fool, because we are thinking other kinds of thoughts. We have the thoughts of God and talk the language of God, which is stupid. That is why Ignatius says that he wants to imitate Jesus "in bearing all wrongs and all abuse and all poverty, both actual and spiritual," should God "choose and admit [him] to such a state and way of life" (no. 98). He got the message. The redemption of the world is achieved on the cross, not in activity, but rather in suffering. Do we want to follow Christ? Then we must enter into the Incarnation in its fullness! We have to identify with the saving act of Christ, which was not his preaching and his miracles, but his cross and resurrection. The moment we live out this doctrine we begin to taste the suffering that it brings and its blessedness at the same time.

[José] Calveras would say to us: "The cross is sweet. That's what we haven't got. The cross is not bitter. This is the great mystery, this is the great sweetness." Scripture references to support his bold statement include 2 Corinthians 1:5; 2 Corinthians 4:7–12; 2 Corinthians 6:3–5; 2 Corinthians 11:20–23; Philippians 1:20; Philippians 3:7–8; Romans 8:31–36.

If the retreatant is ready for this meditation—identifying him- or herself with the saving act of Christ, taking up the cross and being ready to follow him—he or she can go on with the retreat.

We must never seek suffering for its own sake, though. What we are seeking is goodness, truth, and love. Suffering unto itself is an evil; we should never close our eyes to that. If it were not so, then we should spread suffering. Hospitals, therapy—they are here to remove suffering: physical and emotional suffering. We must always work to remove it. Yet we experience forces of evil in this world against which we can do nothing. At times it seems even God is helpless.

And as soon as we want to spread out and live a life of truth and love, these forces will attack us through other human beings. We will be attacked. Now the one who spreads the Gospel, who is identified with Jesus Christ, that person is not afraid of these forces. Jesus brings great joy and inner peace. St. Paul puts it well when he says that since "we are justified by faith, we have peace with God through our Lord Jesus Christ" (Rom. 5:1).

All of this reflection on suffering applies literally at the therapeutic level. What is the greatest obstacle to growth? Pain. Nobody wants pain; yet they are then refusing the cross. Viktor Frankl (1905–1997), a Jewish psychiatrist, used to start his lectures often with the words of Jesus, "Whoever does not take up his cross and follow me is not worthy of me" (Matt. 10:38). If people are to find meaning in life, they have to find meaning in pain. If people are to grow, they have to suffer. If people do not want to suffer, they will never grow. That is the whole message of Fritz Perls, when he says: "You will know that you are a successful therapist when your client begins to hate you," because then the therapist is prodding the client into pain, and he or she wants to avoid it. In other words, the person does not want the cross; so they cannot be saved. It is like the person who is told, "Go out and meet new people," and replies, "Oh, I prefer to sit in my room." That individual wants to be comfortable, but he or she will not grow. Do we want to be happy? We have to pay the price. We can choose between two pains: We can rot with our depressions, loneliness, or we can take the pain of risk. All therapy is painful. All growth is painful.

In one of his letters, St. Francis Xavier, when he talks about his troubles at sea and his seasickness, says: "If one accepts all these hardships for the sake of the Lord as one ought, they are a real refreshment. And they offer matters for many and great consolations. And I believe that those who relish the cross of our Lord find rest when they enter these hardships. And when they run away from these hardships, they die. . . . and I barely feel the hardship." That was the way with the saints. That is why a healthy woman like St. Teresa of Avila could say: "to suffer or to die." This is the message of Ignatius's "joy in suffering."

The Demands of the Kingdom

In the exercise on the "Kingdom of Christ," the summons is addressed to all human beings to be "willing to labor [with Christ]," and so by following him in suffering they will "follow [him] in glory" (no. 95). And the enemies are "sensuality and carnal and worldly love" (no. 97). In addition, there are three categories of people: those who are not interested in the call; those who say yes, all ready for the enterprise, but are not ready to go against the three enemies; and the third category, those who are ready to be like Christ and go against their carnal, sensual, and worldly love.

What does Ignatius mean by carnal love, sensual love, and worldly love? These three are enemies who stop us from finding the will of God. Now these loves are not evil in themselves. They do not have the bad connotation for Ignatius that they have in the English translation. Let's look at each.

Carnal love is love that prompts us to fly from physical and mental labor, anything that tires and fatigues, such as the physical deprivations caused by hunger, thirst, and heat. In other words, it is the love of comfort and bodily well-being. People will never conquer Mount Everest if they are victims of this love.

Sensual love is pampering the senses, a love of satisfying interior and exterior senses. It is pretty similar to carnal love—a flight not only from physical pain, but also from loneliness or emptiness.

Finally, worldly love means loving pomp, show, honor, and approval, and avoiding all humiliations.

Now, says Ignatius, if we want to know the will of God we cannot be victims of these things. They will put a thick layer of dust over our eyes.

Ignatius challenges the retreatant at this stage: "This is the kingdom; this is what the King asks; do you want to follow?" I would literally offer the words of Jesus here for the retreatant's benefit: "For which of you, intending to build a tower, does not first sit down and estimate the cost, to see whether he has enough to complete it? Otherwise, when he has laid a foundation and is not able to finish, all who see it will begin to ridicule him, saying, 'This fellow began to build and was not able to finish'" (Luke 14:28–30). We must calculate our strength. If you are going to build a tower but do not have the strength, then you should go no further. Spend those days in prayer, deep prayer. Do not dabble with all of this; this is dynamite. Maybe we are not ready. This is an important thing to find out.

What are the dangers in all this? One of the dangers here is to embrace suffering for suffering's sake. That is why some people idealize the third degree of humility, which according to Ignatius is the most perfect kind of humility and consists in imitating Christ in all ways, in choosing poverty over riches and insults over honors. It means being considered a fool in the eyes of the world rather than sitting aloft as a person of wisdom and prudence. As Christ was treated in the world, so should we be treated. There can be something dangerous in such a perspective. To accept suffering and hardship for their own sake is perverse.

Next there is the danger of "looking out for self." This creates resentments. This is not what the kingdom is about. The idea can be represented as: "Why am I ready to take up suffering? For the sake of happiness, for the sake of growth, or for the sake of love? Love entails these things, and I want to love fully, so I take these things. If I could have happiness with comfort, even better."

Comfort is not an evil; those three loves are not bad. They are dangerous, that is all, but they are not bad. They are good things. The desire for the approval of others is also a good thing, and that is where we go wrong, because we teach people that it is bad to desire it. It is good, it is healthy, but it is also dangerous if it is our primary motivation.

Another danger is the idea that creatures are bad, and thinking that comforts, entertainment, and the good things of life are bad. This is a kind of a Hindu notion, to want to give up these things. What we truly want is inner freedom from all creature comforts. Yet we are not fully free unless we can take them without guilt; and leave them without compulsion. I could eat a good meal and not feel guilty and enjoy it. That is freedom; I have no compulsion to eat. There are a number of religious who are able to break with compulsion, but they are not able to take some things without guilt. They need training in that. Go to the movies. Go and enjoy them!

Unfortunately the second week and reflections on the kingdom have sometimes led people to be rigid, to take a very negative view of applause, comfort, and positive strokes. This is not the point of the Exercises. The point is not renunciation, but freedom. And we see that in the person of Jesus. He has nowhere to lay his head. He moves from village to village when his work demands this, but not when he is invited to a banquet. We get the impression that he is treating himself well, because compared with John the Baptist, this guy eats and drinks well. (See Luke 7:31–35.)

In addition, we find some psychological dangers in the kingdom contemplation. Novitiates have ruined many young religious psychologically. They are not ready for this. Let them grow little by little. I remember a novice master saying to me: "Where physical hardships are concerned, where humiliations are concerned, I go very slow. All that stupid nonsense of calling them in and humiliating them. You can do them great harm." These people need to grow in the appreciation of themselves. If we are going to die to ourselves for God, we have to have some life already there. For heaven's sake, the poor fellow is not even born and we are killing him already!

We need to encounter each individual where he or she is. It is not a matter of grading. We can never judge who is higher or more pleasing to God. We might never know. So nobody has to be left with an inferior feeling of "Poor me, I am still here." My advice would be that you do your thing right now; that's the best thing you can do. And you are the saintliest of people in doing your thing now. And if your thing is to go to a restaurant and have a good meal, do it and enjoy it. St. Teresa said, "When fasting then fast; when eating chicken, then eat chicken." Or the Zen master: "When I eat, I eat; when I sleep, I sleep." This is the height of spirituality.

THE APPLICATION OF THE SENSES: FANTASY

With this meditation on the kingdom, Ignatius invites the retreatant to tackle problems head-on. What is it that is impeding a person from knowing God's will and carrying it out?
What is it that is impeding people from growing spiritually
and even, one might say, psychologically? It is their carnal
love, sensual love, worldly love. If they can be liberated from
these loves, which are really good but dangerous—the love of
comfort, the love of taking it easy, the love of getting the approval of everyone—then they will be able to see their
destiny and follow it with courage. Just what is the method
for attaining this freedom? It is not enough that the retreatants propose it to themselves. How can they attain this?
How can people be liberated?

The method they should follow is by falling in love with
the person of Christ and with Christ's way of life. Through
Christ's heart Christ will win them over. Then, in the meditations, the technique they must follow is a form of contemplation, fantasy through imagination. That is essentially
what most of the second week is all about. And when we
read those contemplations, we will see that Ignatius did not
care too much about their historical and geographical accu-
racy. History isn't important here. The imagination is key.

Ignatius suggests we imagine the crib in Bethlehem, and
so forth, and then he gives three points as ways of fleshing
out the scene: Consider those present in the fantasy: Where
are they? What are they saying? and What they are doing?
Next we participate in the scenes, so it is a real practice; we
do not stand outside and watch, except in the meditation on
the Incarnation. All this is quite fanciful, which is the point.

It is a matter of living with Christ in fantasy, getting to know him that way, and falling in love with his way of life. This might be journeying with the Lord, sharing his hunger, thirst, heat, cold, and insults before he dies on the cross (see no. 116). Ignatius tells us to watch Christ, see how he lives in freedom from carnal, worldly, and sensual love. Fall in love with him, his way of life, and then our heart will be prepared for what is going to follow: namely, discovering the will of God for ourselves, seeing it unflinchingly, and then following it.

Now people have all kinds of objections to using this method. They say, "Christ is not actually dying today, or born today. How can I imagine myself there?" But so many great saints and mystics have gone in for this. St. Anthony of Padua imagined holding the child Jesus, and he is a doctor of the Church and an outstanding theologian. He was no fool. He knew that Jesus was no longer an infant. St. Francis of Assisi imagined taking Christ down from the Cross; he knew that Jesus was no longer on the cross. St. Teresa of Avila consoled Christ in his Agony in the Garden. What were all these people up to? Did they not know that all these things were not literally taking place? Of course they knew! But they understood truth! This is not so much a truth of history, but *a truth of mystery*. Jesus is no longer an infant, and yet he is! On the rational level, this is hard to explain. On the mystical level, on the level of wisdom, a deep reality abides there, which can only be expressed in these terms, by making believe. When we make believe, it is true: Christ is dying on the cross today; he is an infant once more. This is not in our narrow, discursive way of thinking, but something much deeper.

This has to be tied in with the fifth contemplation for each day of the second week: the application of senses, a very mysterious and very important exercise. First, it seems to be the same as the contemplation, seeing the persons and hearing what they are saying, but then he introduces a new point: "to smell the infinite fragrance, and taste the infinite sweetness of the divinity" (no. 124). It is a kind of letting oneself go in love. Ignatius is very reverent. He does not instruct us to embrace and kiss the person, but the place where the person is.

The most important point, however, is to smell and taste the infinite fragrance and sweetness of the Divinity. What does Ignatius mean by this? These are metaphors, of course. He wants us to experience the infinite consolation that was in the heart of Christ and in his life. Jesus was inundated with a deep peace and happiness. If it is true that no person is so happy as one intimately united with God, then it is also true that Jesus Christ was the happiest person who ever existed in this world. Ignatius wants us to taste that. Because the heart will never be weaned away from its attachments except through something that offers it greater consolation and happiness. We cannot wean ourselves away through mere willpower.

Look at Jesus Christ who is suffering a great deal and still is tremendously happy. Taste that. Ignatius hopes that as a result of this our own hearts will be filled with consolation, and we will say affectively now and not with our willpower pushing us: "I want this! I want to live a simple life. I want to live a poor life. I want to live an independent life. I want to live a life where I am really doing my thing and following the will of the Father for me. I do this because I know this will bring great peace, great strength." When Ignatius has got the retreatant into this frame of mind, he or she is really ready to search for God's will.

When Ignatius talks about smelling and tasting, he talks about a mystical reality. Most mystics express their experience of God in terms of light, sound, fragrance, warmth, or sweetness. How else do we express it except in terms of the senses: the fragrance of God's presence, the warmth of closeness with him, or the melody of the sound he will produce? Here is an example from St. Augustine:

> What do I love when I love my God? Not physical beauty or beauty of a temporal order, not the brilliance of earthly light, so welcome to our eyes, not the sweet melody of harmony and song, not the fragrance of flowers, perfumes, and spices, not limbs such as the body delights to embrace. It is not these that I love when I love my God, and yet, when I love him it is true that I love a light of a certain kind, a voice, a perfume, a food, an embrace. But they are of the kind that I love with my inner self, when my soul is bathed in light that is not bound by space, when it listens to a sound that never dies away, when it is fragrance that is not carried away on the wind, when it tastes food that is never consumed with eating, when it clings to an embrace from which it is not severed by fulfillment of desire. This is what I love when I love my God.

Ignatius says something similar to this:

> It happens sometimes that the Lord himself moves our soul and forces us as it were to this or that particular action by laying our souls wide open. That means that he begins to speak in the very depth of our being, without any clamor of words. He enraptures the soul

completely into his love, and he bestows on us an awareness of himself so that, even if we wished, we would be unable to resist . . . We have, however, been speaking of things which it is impossible to render in words as they really are, or at least not without giving very lengthy and detailed accounts. And even then it would still be a matter which we would better feel inwardly than impart outwardly to others.

Augustine and Ignatius are both speaking of the deep experiences that can only be falteringly expressed in terms of the senses. So this is the first thing to understand here. These are what many mystics call "spiritual senses," which have become blunted by sin. We all have these senses. We could have this kind of experience of God, but somehow these senses have become blunted. For the mystics the soul beholds Christ, hears him, becomes aware of him through his pleasant fragrances, savors him and embraces him, and this can be grasped only by the man who receives this grace of prayer. For it is less a matter of intellectual consideration than of living experience. Thus, at this stage of prayer the soul has now won back the interior senses, so that it may behold the supreme beauty, hear the supreme harmony, breathe in the supreme fragrance, savor the supreme sweetness, and touch the supreme delight.

How do we recover these senses?

First: petitionary prayer. It is a pure grace!

Second: the use of the imaginative senses, fantasy. When we get into the fantasy, going through the life of Christ, something happens in our hearts and we suddenly notice we are tasting spiritual consolation. Spiritual consolation is all of this: taste, fragrance, warmth, and embraces; it really comes

down to that. The application of the senses is a good transition. While we are doing this, the exterior senses are qui-
eted, and then these inner senses have the time and chance
to develop. People who are totally poured out into their exterior senses will never have this develop. That is the reason
that many of the mystics withdraw from exterior life.

How does this transition happen? Ignatius is leading the
retreatant from the exterior senses of fantasy to this deep
inner sense of consolation. The images simplify one's prayer;
reasoning becomes quiet and not very discursive. The retreatant quiets the outer senses. One great mystic says that
when contemplation is born, reason dies; all thinking becomes quiet; there are only images and affection. Now listen
to the words of Christ, to his words through fantasy. Perhaps this plunges a person into complete silence. At this
point, the retreatant is in touch with the wordless sound, a
silence that brings great peace, a wisdom that cannot be explained in words. Or perhaps a person touches and embraces
the feet of Christ—another image—and suddenly she feels a
deep warmth in the heart. She is in touch with God; there is
an experience there. Or again perhaps we imagine Jesus in
front of us, he is looking at us very lovingly, and then all of a
sudden the image disappears and we are only aware of a
presence.

The method of using fantasy is ideally geared toward this.
Sometimes the use of the Jesus Prayer, together with the
image of our Lord present, is also a great help. The disciples
of St. Bernard asked him how he experienced Christ. He
said, "There is nothing sensational. I don't see anything, I
don't hear voices, I suddenly feel a warmth and glow in my
heart and I know that the bridegroom is there, and there are
times when I feel he has gone away, and then I begin to cry

out: 'come back.' I keep crying out till he comes back. That's all my experience."

Keep in mind that Ignatius is using this method to liberate us from being encrusted in our fears, inhibitions, worldly love, carnal love, or sensual love. Ultimately he will use these mystical experiences to get us to see the will of God and do it.

Notice the petition in the second week: "for an intimate knowledge of our Lord, who has become man for me, that I may love him more and follow him more closely" (no. 104). Again it is always in the context of the kingdom. This knowledge of Christ is really an encounter with Christ; it is not knowledge about him, it is a question of meeting him, discovering him, sensing his presence, and being captivated by him as a person. I am always moved by a letter that Gandhi wrote to Stanley Jones, a Protestant evangelist. Jones had written to him:

> You know my love for you and how I try to interpret you and your movement to the West. But I am rather disappointed in one matter. I thought you had grasped the center of the Christian faith, but I am afraid I must change my mind. I think you have grasped certain principles of the Christian faith that have molded you and have helped make you great. You have grasped the principles, but you have missed the person. You said in Calcutta to the missionaries that you did not turn to the Sermon on the Mount for consolation but to the Bhagavad Gita. Neither do I turn to the Sermon of the Mount but to this person who embodies and illustrates the Sermon on the Mount and he is much more. Here is where I think you are weakest in your grasp. May I

suggest that you penetrate through the principles to the person, and come back and tell us what you have found? I do not say this to you as a mere Christian propagandist. I say this because we need you and need the illustration you could give us if you really grasped the center, the person.

When Gandhi got that letter he took his pen and replied that same day:

I appreciate the love underlying the letter and the kind thought for my welfare, but my difficulty is of long standing. Other friends have pointed this out to me before now. I cannot grasp this position by the intellect, the heart must be touched. Saul became Paul not by an intellectual effort but by something touching his heart. All I can say is that my heart is absolutely open, I want to find the truth, to see God face to face.

Splendid. He said: "I am ready, let him touch me." I have this deeply rooted belief that Jesus purposely did not touch him. And this man was very open to Jesus. He was something like Simone Weil. I still believe that God did not want her to enter the Church but to stay where she was. Both these people really grasped what knowing Christ means and put it so well. This is the point of knowing Christ in the Exercises; this is what the retreatant is opening up to when he comes close to Christ; and this experience cannot be produced or coerced. We get to our fantasies and the rest of it, but we ask through petition that Jesus will manifest himself to us in the way it is said in John 14–16: "[W]hoever loves me will be loved by my Father, and I will love him and reveal myself to him" (John 14:21); and "you will grieve, but your grief will become joy . . . But I will see you again, and your hearts will rejoice, and no one will take your joy away from you" (John 16:20, 22). This is grace. This is a gift from God. We have to wait patiently during the retreat to get to this.

Regarding this knowing Christ, it is not possible without an encounter. Ignatius writes in his autobiography: "That woman said, may the Lord Jesus Christ appear to you some day." He was surprised at this and asked, "How will the Lord Jesus Christ appear to me?" But later on he knew exactly what she meant. Very often he had visions of Christ, not intellectual visions, but visions of a tremendous sense of Jesus being present. This is the thing Paul yearns for in Philippians 3:10 ("I want to know Christ and the power of his resurrection and the sharing of his sufferings by becoming like him in death").

This is a mystery that cannot be revealed by mortals (Matt. 11:25–27); this knowing Christ, we cannot produce it (John 17:3–6). We can get the retreatant to pray for this, to pray to the Father that he will make a gift of the retreatant to Jesus Christ (John 6:37). This is the grace Ignatius got at La Storta (a small village just outside Rome), when he asked from the Father to be placed with the Son. The Father said it was his wish that "you take him," a gift the Father made of Ignatius to the Son.

The apostles got this knowledge only gradually and very painfully (Luke 9:45; John 14:9). We should advise the retreatants that we ought not to envy the apostles because they did not yet know Christ; it is obvious from the Gospels. How is this knowledge acquired? By a gift from the Spirit (cf. 1 Cor. 2:11). In fact Ignatius says very movingly in his autobiography, "I did not learn what I know from any man. God taught me as a school master teaches a little child." This is the kind of thing the retreatant has to get in the Exercises. God teaches each one directly. As we hear in the *Exercises*, the Creator deals directly with the creature and "the creature with the Creator" directly; it is not the retreat master who directs people. Rather it is God who does this (no. 15).

I have spoken of the love of Christ, of knowing him, and of that knowledge followed by love in following him. For that love of Christ I give the retreatants Romans 8:35 ("Who will separate us from the love of Christ?"). How marvelous to aspire, to have the ambition to have that kind of love! Of course, Paul is talking of the love Christ has for us, rather than our love for Jesus. In this context of knowing Jesus, loving him, following him, we make those contemplations and applications of senses, then we leave the retreatant be, and it is in this context that he or she will fall in love with God's way and find God's will.

Being Interiorly Free: "The Three Classes of People"

I will beg for the grace to choose what is more
for the glory of the Divine Majesty
and the salvation of my soul.
— IGNATIUS LOYOLA

To choose things only for God and in God we need to be
ready to surrender even seemingly good things. Only that
attitude will bring true freedom and lasting peace.

I want to talk about affective indifference, which is, in a
way, the heart of an Ignatian retreat, specifically the thirty-
day retreat: affective, emotional indifference, because the
whole retreat is geared to help people rid themselves of inordinate attachments. After they have done this, they will
be in a position to seek and find the will of God. This ordinarily happens toward the end of the second week, where
Ignatius proposes an exercise for this: the "Three Classes of
People" (nos. 149–157).

Saving one's soul (no. 150) in the Exercises does not
mean saving one's soul from hell as many have interpreted
it. It would be ridiculous to assert that, as if Ignatius had
said in the "First Principle and Foundation" that "man
[was] created . . . to save himself *from hell*." That would make
no sense. When Ignatius spoke of saving one's soul, he was

speaking of our higher development, our spiritual development and profit, the highest spiritual benefit. When people's
attachments become burdens, they are no longer at peace.
There are attachments that are burdens, and attachments
that are not burdens. When an attachment is "disordered,"
one will never be at peace. When we hold a thing only for
God and in God, then we are always at peace.

THE SECOND AND THIRD CLASSES

We are not interested in the first class of people because
they would like to rid themselves of "the attachment . . . in
order to find peace in God our Lord and assure their salvation, but the hour of death comes, and they have not made
use of any means" (no. 153). It is the second class that interests us. If people want their attachments to be well or-
dered, then the center of gravity of the heart has to be God.
All else should become relativized, just as the love of Mary
for John [the story found in the introduction] does not demand that she give up her love for her parents. No human
being can demand that nor does God demand it. Maybe she
may need to give up their physical presence or their com-
pany, or whatever, but not their love. It is important to understand this second position well, because this is where
many of us fall.

The second class of people "want to rid themselves of
the attachment, but they wish to do so in such a way that
they retain what they have acquired." Let me give an example. I have ten thousand ducats to support me in my old
age, so I cling to this money. I press it to my heart, I cling to
it, and of course this is disordered because I am not holding

it *only* for God. Since my attachment is disordered, what should I do? I will probably beg God, "Please come, send your Holy Spirit into my heart so that I can keep my ten thousand ducats"—to which I am clinging anyway. I am not even ready to consider the possibility of giving them up—so that I could then love those ten thousand ducats with a pure, well-ordered love. This would be a contradiction in terms for Ignatius, because I was not even considering the possibility of giving them up. Ignatius says nothing will happen in such a case.

I remember our Father General [Pedro Arrupe] telling the provincials [Jesuit superiors for a particular geographical area] a couple years ago that he wished all provincials would make the thirty-day retreat again to attain this indifference, because they need to make many decisions today that require a lot of courage. Most people tend to cling to the status quo: keep it, purify their love, but keep it. Should we consider giving up the hospital we have or the school we administer? No. We will keep both but we will do a better job; or we will keep it and purify our love for it, and so on. We do not have the complete freedom of saying: "Give it up, don't give it up; it makes no difference."

I remember once in one of the provinces, the provincial invited the principals of all the schools to make a common discernment on "Should we give up the schools or keep them?" I remember discussing this with a very reputable principal of one of our schools and he told me: "It is ridiculous to consider giving up our schools. We have a commitment to the people for whom we are working." I answered: "I thought our commitment was to Christ, to God. People need to understand that our commitment to them is relative to our primary commitment to God."

He would not even consider the possibility of giving up the schools, and, mind you, he is a man who, if he were told by the provincial tomorrow, "Leave the school and go to a mission station," he would go at the drop of a hat. He was not personally attached to the school. No, he was attached to a value, to a principle, which is just as dangerous. Even if he went to a mission station, he would fight to the death to have that school kept. He was not ready to view the *possibility* of God being more glorified if the school were given up.

It is important to understand the attitude of this second class of men, which is first to cling. Cling to the thing you want and then you can pray to God for all the rest of it: "Make me holy, make me kind, make me love all." I am not denying that a person could become very holy while clinging to an inordinate attachment. He can. He can hold on to his inordinate attachment and still be very holy. I could become a saint, but Ignatius would say "not saint enough." His whole idea was that people could have given God greater glory if they could have loved God the way God wanted and not the way they wanted. Some people say: "Look, I cannot be bothered about greater glory and all that." Ignatius tells us: "Let them go in peace; do not bother. The Exercises are not for them." That is the whole purpose of the "First Principle and Foundation." If people want to find the will of God with complete certitude and clarity, then they must pay a heavy price to know God's will. They must be affectively indifferent even to seemingly good things. So much for the second type of person.

Then comes the third class of man. "They want to rid themselves . . ." The key sentence in this paragraph (no. 155) is: "[T]hey will strive to conduct themselves as if every attachment to it [the ten thousand ducats] had been broken." Let me dramatize this a bit. This man has his ten thousand ducats; he is attached to them; so he prepares himself psychologically. He goes to the retreat master and leaves the ten thousand ducats with him, and, as far as he is concerned, he has given the money up. Has the inordinate attachment gone? No, it has not gone; it is still there because he can still retrieve the money, but he is taking the means to dispose himself. He is ready to act *as if* the money were gone. There is a great psychological value in this. Why? Because we know we always have all kinds of horrors in our imagination that do not exist. Once we actually face the situation, we see that it is not as terrible as we had thought it would be. This frequently happens. We delude ourselves into seeing all types of horrors if we give up the ten thousand ducats, and cannot even face the possibility of giving the money up. Now, if emotionally and psychologically we have given it up and we are acting as if we have given it up, we realize, perhaps, that this is not so bad after all. We are already becoming psychologically indifferent.

This passage has to be read in conjunction with no. 16, where people are urged "to desire the opposite of that to which [the soul] is wrongly attached," to approach it from "the opposite" disposition. Therefore people who love their ten thousand ducats must become disposed to want to give them up. We will soon see how. That is why I told you this [the *Spiritual Exercises*] is a recipe book. Ignatius tells us what to do, how to produce it, how to go about it.

The idea is that we choose something *only* for the glory of God and the benefit of souls. No other reason. Ignatius's first suggestion is that we consider unattractive something that is attractive, and something that is attractive as unattractive. The second suggestion is to ask the Lord for the reverse, for the opposite [of what we desire]. We should pray until the Lord changes our desires. The idea is that we will do nothing until we have changed our attachments; in other words, until the heart is changed. This is what we call surgical prayer. It is painful, but until we have changed our hearts, until we have changed our dispositions and desires, we should not choose anything. As a result the reasons to want or retain anything will be *solely*—the word *solely* is important—for the service, honor, and glory of the Divine Majesty, solely and entirely, not the glory of God *and* my own desires; no, no, *solely* for the glory of God.

PEACE THE RESULT

In the exercise the "Three Classes of People" (no. 157), we read that if we have a repugnance for poverty we should beg the Divine Majesty to choose us for poverty. Ignatius tells us to ask for the things we are afraid of, even to this extent. That is how we change our desires, by asking. We have now done all that is humanly possible to dispose ourselves. No one can be asked to do more. When we love everything in the Creator of them all, then our attachments are purified. What will happen as a result? The third class of man in Ignatius's exercise will hold his ten thousand ducats, but he is no longer attached to them; he is holding them lightly; he is not clinging to them.

He is in a position to ask: "What do you want me to do, Lord? Do you want me to keep them or to give them up?" Then he may hear the Lord saying: "Keep them." Maybe God does not want him to give them up, but now he is attached to something the Lord wanted him to keep anyway, and he is now at peace. The third class of man holds something that the Lord wants him to hold, only because the Lord wants him to hold it and have total peace. The person who reaches this point will take his peace away with him. Whatever happens to people like this, they are peaceful because they have really fallen in love with God; so whatever God arranges is all right. They are always happy, always peaceful; they have found the secret of total and continual joy.

BECOMING PEACEFUL

In our therapy sessions we attempt to clear the ground for happiness; we invite people to be happy, and, as I have told you, many people resist happiness. They do not want to be happy, so they put up all kinds of emotional blocks to happiness. Let us suppose we have psychologically happy people. They still need to get in touch with the Infinite, so that they will achieve these depths of peace. Then nothing can shake them.

I give you the example of St. Ignatius when a doctor told him he did not need to worry about anything. After the doctor had departed, [Pedro] de Ribadeneira, his confidant, asked Ignatius: "Is there anything you worry about?" He was the only one who had the courage to ask Ignatius such questions. Ignatius replied: "No, I do not have anything that might worry me; the only thing that would worry me is if the Society would be suppressed because I am so convinced that God wants it. That would disturb me, but I could even accept that. After fifteen minutes I would be completely at peace." This resolve was put to the test when [Gian Pietro] Caraffa was elected pope. He had previously said he would suppress the Society. It took Ignatius six minutes to become radiant and peaceful again. He was thoroughly upset, but after he went into the chapel, he emerged peaceful, like someone with a mystical sense that everything is in the hands of God. He had no inordinate attachments; he held everything for God. What if God wants to take something away? Great! I always have God. If God wants me to keep it, great! I have God. I am holding it in God. When we are holding something in God, then we are rooted forever.

In this sense the author of the *Imitation of Christ* is right when he says: "He who leans on a creature leans on a reed that is easily broken; he who relies on Jesus remains firm forever" (2.7.3). Who can deny that? It is perfectly true. "The more I am with men, the less of a man I feel" (1.20.1). Who can deny this? As another writer has said, if we do not manage to keep a "coincidence of opposites" in these things, they can do us a lot of harm. We go to an extreme when we jabber, jabber, jabber and think that we are becoming more of a person. But we go to a few cocktail parties and we really come out feeling less human.

FINDING PEACE

Ultimately all comes to finding peace. That was the purpose that Ignatius set out to attain—in particular, in the "Three Classes of People"—to find peace in God our Lord. We will find it only through a painful process.

This process does not exclude preferences. I may prefer

to be a counselor rather than a professor. No, it does not exclude preferences. Basically I am ready to do God's will for God's greater glory. I am ready to become a professor if God so wants. The important thing is that at the moment of making a decision I am unattached. I find happiness in both things. This is the power of consolation. Consolation is really what turns us upside down and transforms us. We can take anything, because somehow we know that, whatever we choose, it will be the will of God and God will be there to console us. Fine, I am ready to take anything, and everything else pales in significance. The other advantages and disadvantages, what do they matter? I know, in one way, I might be more comfortable. But what are comforts when I have God? If we try to attain this on the purely emotional level, it is a perversity. How can we get to the emotional level unless we bring in the spiritual? How do we get to a point where it makes no difference to us to take this or that and be completely at peace regarding both things? If we merely use psychological devices, we may be able to face the situation, but this does not necessarily bring us peace. Our test is whether or not we are perfectly peaceful; whether or not we have courage and joy and peace.

We should not make a decision until we are free. We should make the decision in the context of true freedom. When consolation comes, we are realized, the fears are gone, and the attachments are gone. We are free. For the time being I am not concerned about decisions we need to make in three minutes. The point I am trying to make is that we cannot make any important decision until we have this disposition of freedom. This disposition is essential.

What people often do to find the will of God is to make two columns, reasons for and reasons against a certain decision. This procedure makes no sense; we have lots of spade-work to do first. Even those reasons would be biased. Ignatius said that most decisions cannot be made according to reason. They cannot, because we will find equally good reasons on both sides. We must make them with a certain instinct of the heart.

"Elections"—Making Life Decisions

God our Lord can so move and attract the will that
a devout soul without hesitations follows what has
been manifested to it.
—IGNATIUS LOYOLA

De Mello reflects on two famous passages from The
Spiritual Exercises: *the meditation on the "Two Standards"*
and the consideration on the "Three Degrees or Kinds of
Humility," which help us put aside vested interests and seek
the will of God in making important choices in life with
genuine freedom.

For four or five days in the second week the retreatant is left
by Ignatius to spend time chiefly with the infancy meditations. He or she is supposed to be inundated with great delight, living the hidden life with Christ, Mary, and Joseph,
experiencing the sweetness of their simple existence, their
poverty, and their utter dependence on God. Usually the retreatant has great consolations; he or she finds the meditations very beautiful and moving. After some time in these
meditations the director says: "Now let's work. We start with
the elections [or life decisions]—that is what we came here
for—to find God's will." So there is a kind of break before the
contemplations continue on the public life of Christ. Now

St. Ignatius introduces something to which he gives great importance and many pages—this whole matter of the elections, the purpose of the Exercises, to get rid of inordinate attachments and then to seek and find the will of God.

GETTING RID OF INORDINATE ATTACHMENTS

The great obstacle to knowing God's will is our inordinate attachments. Otherwise it is not so difficult to find God's will. If we do not let smoke screens deceive us, we will see God's will with fair enough clarity. But we suffer from carnal love, sensual love, and worldly love; we have vested interests, and anyone who has vested interests will let them influence his or her thinking.

How do we get rid of these inordinate attachments? Most people won't even see that these attachments are inordinate; they will see them as very good, even very wonderful, and they will find lots of reasons to convince themselves that they are very good. They will even develop a set of reasons, a set of defenses to protect them.

So if I want my job and my car or want to stay right in the place where I am, oh then I have got lots of reasons. I will put a whole wall around that objective to defend it, a wall of reasons. Now the worst thing we can do with these people is to try to argue with them. It is like quicksand: The more we try to get them out of it, the deeper they go in; the more we try to push, the stronger their defenses become; the more we attack them, the more reasons they find; and the more reasons they find, the more they convince themselves. So the best thing to do is stop pushing.

Ignatius uses a tactic, not by arguing with them but by the

only way he can get at them: the way of the heart. Ignatius will make people fall in love with Christ—mysteriously, irrationally, fall in love with the way of Christ, so that now irrationally, they love poverty and humiliations and are ready to take up all the hardships of the Cross. They want to follow Christ in this simplicity of life and are ready to give up everything, so that they might see all those things in a new light. We see the life of Christ and how he saved the world without any show and without any pomp, and we say: "This is what I want." When we say this, we are more detached. We are indifferent. We cannot argue with the retreatants; they have to see the light for themselves and, if they throw themselves into doing the Exercises in this way, if they plunge into them, their defensiveness drops, and then they see things in a true light. So this is the tactic of Ignatius. How do we do it? Ignatius recommends a number of things.

First, Ignatius introduces a consideration about different states of life to "ask in what kind of life or in what state his Divine Majesty wishes to make use of us" (no. 135). All the meditations that follow, including the "Two Standards" and "Three Degrees or Kinds of Humility," are all election meditations. But there is a challenge: How can one make a correct election if one's thinking is wrong? A person's thinking has to be correct, depending on his or her philosophy, thinking, or chosen frame of reference. If people share the thinking of the Second Vatican Council (1962–1965), they will make one decision. If they share the thinking of the First Vatican Council (1869–1870) or the Council of Trent (1545–1563), they will make another decision. If they are capitalists, they will make one decision in regard to developing countries. If they are communists, they will make another decision in regard to boosting the economy of the developing countries. It all depends on people's thinking, including their values and philosophy of life. If they do not have a philosophy in keeping with the life of Christ, they will not make decisions in keeping with the mind of Christ. So the meditation of the "Two Standards" is meant to give us the mind of Christ, the thinking of Christ, by considering "that Christ calls and wants all beneath his standard, and Lucifer, on the other hand, wants all under his" (no. 137).

That is why St. Ignatius proposes a kind of a parable inviting retreatants "to ask for a knowledge of the deceits of the rebel chief and help to guard myself against them; and also to ask for a knowledge of the true life exemplified in the sovereign and true commander, and the grace to imitate him" (no. 139). Then he presents on the one side the devil addressing all his followers. How will he tempt them? Riches, honor, and pride! Here Ignatius is dealing with second-week people who are men and women totally generous to God, ready to do anything for Christ. So the only way the devil can tempt them is by presenting them with something seemingly good. He does not tempt them to anger or to killing people; he has to tempt them under the appearance of good. Riches and honor are neutral things, and Ignatius warns us that the devil will snare us by making us accept something that is apparently good.

Jesus uses very strong words in the Gospel: "You cannot serve God and wealth" (Matt. 6:24). Jesus is not against money, but against loving money and trusting money. Jesus is very, very strong on this point: No rich person will enter heaven. We cannot love two masters; if we love money then automatically we are against God. If we love money, we cannot say we love God, because we do not and we are fooling ourselves. Now money does not necessarily mean material possessions or physical rupees. Here money means anything that helps us to get honors, a means to honors and not necessarily to comfort. "Money" could be one's degree or one's career: such "money" can lead to honors and then to pride.

Here we see the whole matter of true security, of relying only on God and not on anything else; this is the perfection Jesus demands in the Gospel. Those "Two Standards" are the quintessence of the Sermon on the Mount. In fact, this section of the Gospel can be given to the retreatants instead of the "Two Standards"— repent and believe the joyful news. How happy are those who are poor, those with no influence, those who are really helpless and depending only on God; these are happy people, even now, happy people. This is a mysterious, completely different set of values. As one author says, everything that the world counts as a blessing, Jesus counts as a curse; on the other hand, everything that the world counts as a curse, Jesus counts as a blessing. We have to confront the retreatant with this joyful news. The kingdom has come and Ignatius wants the retreatant to get a sense of that and of the dangers contained in money and honors.

In the Sermon on the Mount, we see Jesus gathering the apostles around him and sending them out with the instructions:

> And preach as you go, saying, "The kingdom of heaven is at hand." Heal the sick, raise the dead, cleanse lepers, cast out demons. You received without paying, give without pay. Take no gold, nor silver, nor copper in your belts, no bag for your journey, nor two tunics, nor sandals, nor a staff; for the laborer deserves

his food. And whatever town or village you enter, find out who is worthy in it, and stay with him until you depart. As you enter the house, salute it. And if the house is worthy, let your peace come upon it; but if it is not worthy, let your peace return to you. And if any one will not receive you or listen to your words, shake off the dust from your feet as you leave that house or town. Truly, I say to you, it shall be more tolerable on the day of judgment for the land of Sodom and Gomor'rah than for that town. Behold, I send you out as sheep in the midst of wolves; so be wise as serpents and innocent as doves. Beware of men; for they will deliver you up to councils, and flog you in their synagogues, and you will be dragged before governors and kings for my sake, to bear testimony before them and the Gentiles. When they deliver you up, do not be anxious how you are to speak or what you are to say; for what you are to say will be given to you in that hour; for it is not you who speak, but the Spirit of your Father speaking through you. Brother will deliver up brother to death, and the father his child, and children will rise against parents and have them put to death; and you will be hated by all for my name's sake. But he who endures to the end will be saved. When they persecute you in one town, flee to the next; for truly, I say to you, you will not have gone through all the towns of Israel, before the Son of man comes. A disciple is not above his teacher, nor a servant above his master; it is enough for the disciple to be like his teacher, and the servant like his master. If they have called the master of the house Be-el'zebul, how much more will they malign those of his household. So have no fear of them; for nothing is covered that will not be revealed, or hidden that will not be known. What I tell you in the dark, utter in the light; and what you hear whispered, proclaim upon the housetops. And do not fear those who kill the body but cannot kill the soul; rather fear him who can destroy both soul and body in hell. Are not two sparrows sold for a penny? And not one of them will fall to the ground without your Father's will. But even the hairs of your head are all numbered. Fear not, therefore; you are of more value than many sparrows. So every one who acknowledges me before men, I also will acknowledge before my Father who is in heaven; but whoever denies me before men, I also will deny before my Father who is in heaven. Do not think that I have come to bring peace on earth; I have not come to bring peace, but a sword. For I have come to set a man against his father, and a daughter against her mother, and a daughter-in-law against her mother-in-law; and a man's foes will be those of his own household. He who loves father or mother more than me is not worthy of me; and he who loves son or daughter more than me is not worthy of me; and he who does not take his cross and follow me is not worthy of me. He who finds his life will lose it, and he who loses his life for my sake will find it. He who receives you receives me, and he who receives me receives him who sent me. He who receives a prophet because he is a prophet shall receive a prophet's reward, and he who receives a righteous man because he is a righteous man shall receive a righteous man's reward. And whoever gives to one of these little ones even a cup of cold water because he is a disciple, truly, I say to you, he shall not lose his reward. (Matt. 10:7–42).

If we do not have these values, it is useless to go ahead with the retreat; and many retreatants do not have these values. We have to pick up the values of the Sermon on the Mount and of Jesus' instructions to the apostles. Still, even if we have these values, the heart may still be attached. This is where we get rid of our inordinate attachments and prayer becomes surgical prayer. It can be painful. Some people say prayer is an escape. When people say prayer is an "escape," I say: "Yes? Have you ever tried it?" And usually they have not. If we try to get them to pray for one hour every day, they will not; they would rather read a novel. If prayer is really what it should be, it is a painful experience because we are reporting for orders. That is the way a person encounters God, the God of the Bible.

The God of the Bible is always encountered in a command. He is always saying "Come"; he is always saying "Go"; he is always saying "Do." Abraham, Moses, the Prophets, Our Lady, Jesus Christ—God calls each one by his or her name. Many of us don't want to hear it. Moses says, "Call Aaron, not me." Jeremiah is always running away. God does not say that anyone will do; he grips us and *wants us*. Our vocation is never for ourselves but always for others. It is always in a command. And sooner or later we will hear the command, and we will get frightened. This is what happens in the Exercises; we have got to hear that voice and follow God, wherever he leads, whatever is our destiny. Follow him. Here is where prayer becomes difficult, when we are confronted with the commands of God. Yet, frightening as it is, if we surrender to these orders, then all is well and nothing can disturb our peace.

THREE DEGREES OF HUMILITY

According to Ignatius, there are three degrees of humility. First, those who avoid mortal sin. Second, those who have resolved never to commit a venial sin for anything in the world. Third, those who have embraced the "First Principle and Foundation," who choose "what is more conducive to the end for which we are created" (no. 23). These people have arrived.

Yet, even in *this third degree of humility*, when we have so much love for Christ, there is still a possibility that we might deceive ourselves. Ignatius is very wary of self-deception. Our hearts have to be touched so that we would rather choose the path that Christ chose than any other. This is not suffering for suffering's sake. It is not that, faced with two things, we choose what is more difficult. That would be immoral, because we cannot canonize the difficult for the sake of the difficulty. That would hold no value. Such an approach would not be Christianity, but rather Stoicism or masochism. Nevertheless, that is how some of our rules have been interpreted: "constant mortification, continual abnegation," and so on. From my perspective, "mortification" comes from the word *mors*, which is not *mutilation* but *death*, a death achieved in love, when we love to die. When we love totally, we die totally. We can also claim that we live totally, which is also true. Mortification that is built not on love but on self-mutilation is very dangerous.

Now let me tell you the way I see this continual mortification and continual abnegation. People may have to choose between going to a movie and going to Benediction of the Blessed Sacrament. They say, "I'd rather go to the movie because I enjoy movies and don't enjoy Benediction. Good, then I'll be more perfect if I go for Benediction because I don't like it." This is not mortification. This is the act of a person who hates himself or herself and is self-mutilating. Real mortification is the act of a dead person, one who is totally dead to oneself and who is totally in love with God. This person will face Christ and ask, "Which do you prefer?" Christ may say, "I prefer that you go to the movie." The person then responds: "Gee, I'll go to the movie," and she will enjoy it. She is mortifying herself. This is the act of a dead person fully alive in Christ. Whereas the other person, who acts without any reference to Christ and does what does not please him, is really not mortified at all. He is not dead. So the truly mortified person is the "dead" person who has died totally in love for Christ. She has asked him: "What do you want? Whatever you want, I'll do. Whatever gives you delight gives me delight."

Let us begin with Ignatius's remark about not "giving cause" for such humiliations. Once there was a novice who went to see St. Teresa of Avila and asked if she could say stupid things at recreation so that she would be humiliated. St. Teresa asked: "More stupid things?" And the novice was very hurt! Joseph Rickaby wrote, "Don't make an attempt to make a fool of yourself, but be resigned when you are found out." So Ignatius tells us not to give cause for being humiliated, but when we are "found out," to rejoice.

The author of *The Cloud of Unknowing* says that when the blind stirring of love begins to grip our hearts powerfully, we become helpless. We are pulled by love, we are pushed by love, we can do nothing except what it pushes us to do. Surrender in love completely—surrender the whole of ourselves to that blind stirring of love—is what Ignatius talks about in the third degree of humility. It is *not* an attitude of choosing what is more difficult, what is more painful, what is more crucifying. Rather let us choose what is more conducive to the end for which we are created. Let us choose what is more pleasing to God; that is the aim. And it is a great pity that this third degree of humility has been taken out of its context to canonize the unpleasant, the hard, and the painful: this is unhealthy spirituality.

COMMENTS ON MAKING DECISIONS

Ignatius gives us clear instructions on how to go about deliberating and finding out what God wants of us. Let us imagine some people who are considering whether they should become a religious or not, or take up this job or not. First, Ignatius tells them: "In every good choice, as far as depends on us, our intention must be simple. I must consider only the end for which I am created, that is, for the praise of God our Lord and for the salvation of my soul. Hence, whatever I choose must help me to this end for which I am created" (no. 169). So the intention has to be simply "What do you want, God?" One should not say: "I want the glory of God and the welfare of the Church," or "the glory of God and the welfare of the nation," or "my health." No, the intention should be only the glory of God, nothing else. All other things will only confuse the issue.

Now, this can be difficult to accept. As I said before, one person's intention may be the "welfare of my nation." Maybe God wants the nation to cease to exist. Nations have risen and died out in the past. "What about the glory of the Church?" Forget the glory of the Church. Maybe God wants the Church to be humiliated and to die in a particular way? So keep the Church out of this. Do not equate the Church with God! And one's health has absolutely nothing to do with the question, because maybe God wants a person to have ill health. Very often our intentions are not simple and then we do not find God's will. What I should intend is God's glory, nothing else.

Furthermore, I must not subject and fit the end to the means, but the means to the end. So not only must my intention be simple, but *it has to be pure*. What does that mean? It is not that I first choose something and then I want the maximum glory of God. No, I want the glory of God before I choose anything, then the question should simply be: "Am I to become a religious or get married?"—not "Oh, I will get married and then seek the glory of God." One needs total indifference.

What can we choose? What are subjects for election? We make an election about something where both sides are pleasing to God, where neither side is commanded or forbidden. If something is commanded or forbidden, the will of God is clear. Let me quote the words of Ignatius:

> It is necessary that all matters of which we wish to make a choice be either indifferent or good in themselves, and such that they are lawful within our Holy Mother, the hierarchical Church, and not bad or opposed to her. (no. 170)

> There are things that fall under an unchangeable choice, such as the priesthood, marriage, etc. There are others with regard to which our choice may be changed, for example, to accept or relinquish a benefice, to receive or renounce temporal goods. (no. 171)

With regard to an *unchangeable* choice, once it has been made, for instance, by marriage or the priesthood, etc., since it cannot be undone, no further choice is possible. Only this is to be noted. If the choice has not been made as it should have been, and with due order, that is, if it was not made without inordinate attachments, one should be sorry for this, and take care to live well in the life he has chosen.

Since such a choice was inordinate and awry, it does not seem to be a vocation from God, as many erroneously believe. [Some people try to] make a divine call out of a perverse and wicked choice. For every vocation that comes from God is always pure and undefiled, uninfluenced by the flesh or any inordinate attachment. (no. 172)

Then Ignatius comments on choices already made about matters that in principle could be changed: "In matters that *may be changed*, if one has made a choice properly and with due order, without any yielding to the flesh or the world, there seems to be no reason why he should make it over. But let him perfect himself as much as possible in the one he has made" (no. 173). The idea is that once a person has made a choice and gone through all the motions of finding the will of God, he or she should stick to the choice, unless there is clear evidence that the question should be reopened.

This clear evidence can come either from the fact that the retreatant omitted a piece of evidence when he or she was making the choice, or it can come from the discernment of spirits when the person is troubled. Notice here a clear pull to something else. That is why I tell people not to make this as an exercise in futility. If God wants something, he will make it pretty clear to us. One of the ways he does that is to make us feel uneasy about the choice we made. Then it is time to start. A person does not need to make a vocation retreat every retreat. I chose this way of life, and it seems to me I chose it well. Now let God take the initiative if he wants me to get out of it. God must take the initiative. Once people have made the decision, they should offer it to God and move ahead unless they stumble on a piece of evidence that they have not noticed before.

Now comes the more delicate and important part of this whole business when Ignatius speaks of "three times when a correct and good choice of a way of life may be made" (no. 175). These "times" are not temporal constructs: hours, days, or weeks, but three dispositions of the heart and soul, within which one can find out God's will.

First time: "When God our Lord so moves and attracts the will that a devout soul without hesitation, or the possibility of hesitation, follows what has been manifested to it. St. Paul and St. Matthew acted thus in following Christ our Lord" (no. 175). This was in Ignatius's day probably the most common way in which people found out their vocation. God starts pulling; he attracts. In such a case, a person has not lost his or her liberty. As theologians say, God can make us do something freely. We are just pulled, and we follow.

Second time: "When much light and understanding are derived through experience of desolations and consolations and discernment of diverse spirits" (no. 176). There are moments when I am in consolation and moments when I am in desolation. Then I start discerning. This is God's language:

consolation and desolation. God is indeed saying something.

Third time: "This is a time of tranquillity. One considers first for what purpose man is born, that is, for the praise of God our Lord and for the salvation of his soul. With the desire to attain this before his mind, he chooses as a means to this end a kind of life or state within the bounds of the Church that will be a help in the service of his Lord and for the salvation of his soul. I said it is a time of tranquillity, that is, a time when the soul is not agitated by different spirits, and has free and peaceful use of its natural powers" (no. 177).

Conspicuously absent during this time for finding God's will is the time of desolation. We find out God's will when we are pulled and attracted: that is, through a powerful consolation. Second, we find God's will through experiencing consolations and desolations and then interpreting them. In consolation we are at peace. In desolation we never find out God's will. This is a valuable thing to know. People may come to consult about their vocations when they are troubled, agitated, and depressed. This is no time to reopen anything. Wait till they are peaceful, calm, and happy. Then reopen the question, if they want to. "[I]n desolation the evil spirit guides and counsels" (no. 318). So never make a decision in desolation.

GOD'S WILL IN SMALL THINGS

Ignatius asks us in the *Constitutions of the Society of Jesus* to seek the will of God not only in the choice of life, but in all particulars. Can we find out God's will even in trifles? Is it possible? Yes and no. If we do it purely on the level of reason or asceticism, it is impossible. If we have the grace of which the author of *The Cloud of Unknowing* speaks, if we are gripped by this blind stirring of love, and we instinctively know what we should be doing, *then it is possible.* There are times, however, when it is possible even on the ascetical, reasoning level. For example, I could write a letter or read a novel. What is more pleasing to God? Am I really indifferent? By asking this, we often get the light; we see where we are fooling ourselves. Of course, all this presupposes a healthy personality. If we are all tied up with our "drives," this approach will not work.

What if a person makes a decision without making all these elections? Should he or she reopen the question? Only if there is evidence to reopen the question. If God wants us somewhere else, he will do something to make us reopen the question either through consolation or desolation or through some event in our life. An event comes into one's life and the person wonders, "Am I in the right place?" And he reopens the question. For example, a scholastic [a Jesuit in training who has not taken final vows] who falls in love might be in such a position. I would see the legitimacy of the fact that here comes a new event in my life, a new experience of which I knew nothing, which would justify my reopening the question of vocation. One should be ready for that possibility.

Discernment of Spirits

*It is characteristic of the good spirit to give
courage and strength, consolation, tears,
inspiration, and peace.*
—IGNATIUS LOYOLA

*De Mello expounds on guidelines for understanding various
movements and emotions that affect the human heart.
Where, in the ebb and flow of these movements, can I find
the will of God?*

THE HEART OF THE EXERCISES

Ignatius introduces "[r]ules for understanding to some extent
the different movements produced in the soul and for recognizing those that are good, to admit them, and those that are
bad, to reject them" (no. 313). The discernment of spirits pi-
lots within our heart a kind of ebb and flow of movements
through which we can find the will of God. It is here that the
whole spiritual life is lived. If we are not in touch with all
this, then we are living at a very superficial level in our mind
and will.

This way [of understanding movements within one's

heart] characterizes spiritually mature persons. Such people are aware and do not have repressed feelings. The neurotic, for instance, is a person with repressed feelings. A healthy person does not repress feelings and is completely attuned to inner feelings. In general, the more people are aware of their real feelings, the more transparent and healthier they become.

The more we grow in spiritual maturity, the more we are aware of those movements that are going on deep down within us. We get more sensitized to messages and impulses that keep coming to us, and we can distinguish them. We develop a tremendous sense of "here is a consolation and yet it is suspect, I am mildly uneasy." St. Thomas Aquinas says somewhere: "Just as the bee is led by instinct, not by the mind, so the spiritual person is led by the *spirit*, not by the mind."

When we are led by "the spirit," it will frequently break the rules of our "mind." Ignatius once said to Pedro de Ribadeneira: "In matters of great moment we must push aside human prudence, and open ourselves completely to the Spirit." In this he showed his prophetic genius; outstanding people sooner or later go against human prudence. They take prudence into consideration, but then their instinct moves them. It is essential to get in touch with and discern our spiritual instinct.

SPIRITUAL MOVEMENTS AND MERE EMOTIONS

How do we define a spiritual movement as opposed to a mere emotion? It is important to distinguish, because a spiritual movement has repercussions *in our emotions*, while forming a stage *beyond the emotions*. It tastes like nothing; it feels like nothing; we do not know it directly but only through its effects. In itself it is emptiness, nothingness, spirit. And spirit has no form, no feeling, no thought, nothing.

How then do we distinguish between mere emotional states and spiritual movements? How do we distinguish, for instance, euphoria from spiritual consolation, depression from spiritual desolation? Discernment is learned in the depths of one's heart, in silence, in long exposure to prayer and to the Bible and in suffering. Only by sharing God's mentality and Christ's mentality do we develop an instinct for what is right and wrong, where the Spirit is speaking and where not. Like a taste for music, good painting, and wine, we develop an instinct for discernment and do not learn through books and seminars. We learn discernment through probing the depths of our hearts.

RULES FOR UNDERSTANDING AND THE IMPORTANCE OF THE SPIRITUAL DIRECTOR

In his "Rules for the Discernment of Spirits" Ignatius writes of "rules for understanding to some extent the different movements produced in the soul" (no. 313). Yet we can never understand discernment through rules. Discernment is communicated by the Holy Spirit. So why do we have to understand these rules? For one thing, so that we can admit the good spirits and reject the bad spirits. That is the whole purpose of these rules. We can do something about these movements. First of all, the rules are a language. Something is being said to us and communicated to us. It is important to pick up those messages. There are good movements that we foster, harbor, join, and take in. In contrast, there are bad movements that we resist and against which we are on the alert.

When we apply these rules, we have to find out first the kind of person to whom we are applying them. One principle is that whatever causes sadness comes from the devil, not from God. So when we pick up sadness we might say that this could not be from God. But do not be too fast in applying this common principle. We must proceed with caution. A person who goes from one mortal sin to another and is completely dead spiritually might come to us and say, "There are moments of deep sadness in my life, something that makes me uneasy." This could be the good spirit. In this kind of person, as Ignatius says, the good spirit "will rouse the sting of conscience and fill them with remorse," whereas the evil spirit will make that person feel at ease and happy (no. 314).

Many psychological things can be mixed up here. We need great sophistication and subtlety to deal with such cases. This is a wisdom that comes from knowing a lot of psychology.

Some people might say: "Don't give us psychology, give us spirituality." That makes me think of a fellow I once met who went on discerning under a great master for weeks and weeks about whether he should continue in the Society of Jesus or not. Then he came to the conclusion that he should stay because of this movement and that, this spirit and that, and he was in great consolation.

Next he went off to his counselor, who said, "You are hungry and are insecure. Are you aware of this?" The fellow then got in touch with his hunger and insecurity and realized: "This life is not for me. I need a woman." So he went and got married with my blessing. There had been weeks of discernment, but they were all wasted. I am not saying that this fellow could not have found the will of God through discernment. What I want to suggest is that the spiritual director lacked wisdom in guiding him, and did not identify his desolation as depression, his consolation as euphoria. Meanwhile, the man was repressing his feelings all the time. When we come with a problem of love, love for a woman or a man, then I want to know exactly what the retreatant is feeling, before he or she covers the whole thing up. Lots of wisdom is needed in all of this.

WHAT DO INDIVIDUALS WANT?

Before we find out what God wants, let us find out what the individual wants! We need to know what the person feels like doing. There is plenty of time to find out what God wants. The general rule I give to people is to find out what they want to do, namely something that fits in with their interests and talents. It is as if God created them for this. Go ahead and do it. He has given them the inclinations, the talents, the joy in doing it. I am open to the fact that God may not want them to do it. Just bring me the evidence. It is like Jesus saying, "Abba, Father, for you all things are possible; remove this cup from me; yet, not what I want, but what you want" (see Mark 14:36). God may want them to sacrifice something and not take it up. Let us be clear here: I am not denying the spiritual. I am merely saying, "Do not jump to the spiritual before you have gone through the normal way in which God manifests his will." If I were the provincial, the first thing I would say to my subjects is "What would you like to do? What do you enjoy doing the most? And I promise you one thing, I will bend over backward to give it to you, because I see in that the indication of God's will."

I assume that God speaks through all people who have these inclinations, likes, and dislikes. I would challenge them: "Is this what you really want? Is it not a fad? Go to your counselor and spiritual director and find out." After that has been found out, God may speak to me through this. "See, I gave John those talents to use for my kingdom." Then you might say in return, "But our policy in the province . . ." We can change the policy! The policy is the people God has given us. God gave these people a vocation and sent them to us with their talents. But we will weigh their talents against the works to which we are already committed. Yes, we will weigh everything. And then maybe they will have to sacrifice their talents.

Why did God send them here with those talents? We have to ask ourselves that question. Maybe we will adapt the whole province to suit their talents? Remember I am asking, "Are those really his talents? Is that really what he wants?" As Ignatius says, "The God of nature is not different from the God of supernature." God is one and works through all this.

Growth through renunciation comes through life, through situations, through destiny, and through God acting. Do not interpret what I am saying in a naïve way: "Let them each do whatever they like." Certainly not! We Jesuits are a group. We have communal commitments; we have group commitments. For this reason, we must weigh everything against the group commitment. One might have to say to a person, "See, you have a personal charism and could do tremendous work, but we can't fit it in here." So we will take this as an indication of God's will. I admired one provincial, who—already fifteen years ago—asked every Jesuit in his province to write down the three ministries that he would like to do best. He told them: "Find out what you want and rank the results: first, second, third. I cannot promise to follow your indications, but I will try my best." Remember this is discernment, God speaking through the community.

There is a difference between real personal fulfillment and merely satisfying oneself. That is why I say find out what they want. There might be tension in one's life; perhaps a person does not know what to choose given two alternatives; we need help to explore what we really want; there are many factors in our lives to take into account before we decide. Perhaps a person will come out with what he wants and finds it very difficult to fit it in with the work in his province. This would be a real shame!

The main point here is the need to be open to the human situation in every problem that comes up for discernment. This human situation is not quite as human as we think; it is also divine. The human is divine; God is in the human! Explore that!

Desolation and Consolation

In the case of those who go on earnestly striving to cleanse their souls from sin and who seek to rise in the service of God our Lord to greater perfection, the method pursued is the opposite of that mentioned in the first rule.

Then it is characteristic of the evil spirit to harass

with anxiety, to afflict with sadness, to raise obstacles
backed by fallacious reasonings that disturb the soul.
Thus he seeks to prevent the soul from advancing.

It is characteristic of the good spirit, however, to
give courage and strength, consolations, tears, inspirations, and peace. This he does by making all easy, by
removing all obstacles so that the soul goes forward in
doing good. (no. 315)

This is the type of person who is enthusiastically going
all out, who is launching out fully, and who is giving himself or herself completely to God. We are not talking here
about in-between people because they will not come to us
with these problems. Ignatius has spoken of someone who
is a tremendous sinner (no. 314); he speaks now of someone who is doing everything possible to become a saint.
The devil "raises obstacles backed by fallacious reasoning."
Listen here, with the bad person, it is *the good angel who uses
reasoning*, but with the good one, it is *the devil who uses
reasoning*—fallacious, misleading reasoning.

For the spiritual director this is extremely important.
When people come with desolations, there seems no way out
of them. The devil has a Ph.D. in perfect logic. They will say
something like this: "I feel discouraged and depressed. When
I look back, I see how I have wasted my life. I have done
nothing."

You might say: "But discouragement will get you nowhere;
you have to look to the future."

"That's true," they'll say, "but what guarantee do I have
that I will succeed in the future? You want me to trust in
God? I've made thirty-seven retreats up to now and in every

one of them I trusted in God. And I have done a pretty poor job of it. I have no guarantee that the thirty-eighth retreat is going to succeed better."

This fellow may be suffering from psychological depression or from spiritual desolation. But such a person will not get out of the situation through arguments. Do not argue with the devil. Do something else.

Such thoughts could be connected with either consolation or desolation. For instance, "I have wasted my life, and I feel *so consoled* about it." That's a good spirit! Ignatius once wrote to St. Francis Borgia (1510–1572), "The more I see myself, the more I see myself as an obstacle. I see the whole of myself as an obstacle to God's work. This consideration brings me the greatest and sweetest consolation, because I realize that God in his loveliness works so many good things through me."

But I could see "the whole of myself as an obstacle" and become depressed. It is the same thought but a different reaction. One person might say, "Look at the way things are going in the Church now. It is horrible," and the person is all depressed. Another person could say the very same thing, and be all optimistic and ready to do something. The important thing is not what the individuals say, *but their reaction to it*. As I mentioned earlier, Blessed Peter Faber would say: "Even if the Holy Spirit scolds, he scolds you so gently, so sweetly." If somebody comes and says, "God showed me what a sinner I am and how badly I am doing, and I feel depressed," it is not God who has administered that scolding, that is for sure! Because when God administers a scolding, *we feel deeply consoled and peaceful!*

"[I]t is characteristic of the good spirit," Ignatius observes, "to give courage and strength, consolations, tears, inspirations, and peace" (no. 315). For centuries we opposed all these things that Ignatius says are caused by the good spirit. We were told, "Don't ask for consolations. Don't desire consolations. Don't rest in consolations; they come and go." But it is typical of the good spirit to give these things. "This he does by making all easy, by removing all obstacles so that the soul goes forward in doing good" (no. 315). What happens is this: We come to a point where everything is so easy. There are no obstacles, we just fly ahead.

We have had a kind of Pelagian attitude toward these things. A pretty accurate parody of the whole thing would be like this: Here I have a novice who is full of fervor and is moving ahead beautifully. The person is full of consolation and generosity in helping others. He or she is all aglow. Then I say to myself: "This is not a real conversion; you can't rely on that consolation." So I tell the novice, "Don't rely too much on these things. The important thing is meditation, willpower, resolutions. Let's see what happens when this consolation goes." So I suggest to the person not to lean too much on these good feelings, because they come and they go. "You have to lean more on yourself, on building up your strength, so that when this consolation goes, you are still strong." As a result of this, the novice does not take in all the benefits that this consolation could give. Instead of surrendering to it and enjoying it fully, the person is taught to suspect it. This is the way most of us were brought up.

Imagine the wind is in our sails and so the boat is gliding along beautifully, very smoothly. And we say, "Don't rely on that, because the wind will drop. What we want is steady progress. So furl up the sails and row. And keep rowing." And we go on rowing all our lives and we progress about ten feet. Pelagian! The attitude that Ignatius takes is rather this: We have got the consolation, surrender to it. Give in to it completely, because we will travel miles and miles; go right ahead. Then the wind drops. What to do? Pick up your oars? No, start praying, asking for the consolation to come back! Of course, we need to examine ourselves: "Where did I go wrong?" Change what went wrong. Consolation will soon return. Wait for the wind; it will come back. It is only in consolation that we really make progress in true and solid spiritual virtues.

Ignatius made another very strong statement to St. Francis Borgia: "Knowing within ourselves that without these consolations all our thoughts, words, and actions are tainted, cold and disordered, we ask for them so that with them we may become pure, warm, and upright." The situation is good only inasmuch as it is flooded with consolation. So ask for it. Vinoba Bhave says very nicely: "Have you noticed how you keep dragging a boat along the sand? It's so heavy, fifty men can hardly pull it, and then the tide comes in, and two children can pull that boat." This is what happens when God's grace floods into our hearts. Everything becomes so easy. The good spirit makes it all so easy. That is what the whole spiritual life is about! The spiritual life is a kind of romance, in which God plays hide-and-seek. He hides and we search for him; then he comes back and everything is all right. Then once again he hides. This is the spiritual life. It is not an exercise of ascetical willpower, as if I do this and keep progressing. Keeping numbers, accounts, and so forth is not the spiritual life at all. When consolations go away, sit down or kneel down and ask the spirit to come back. A person might say, "Then I have no merit." Precisely! We have no merits and we are nothing; God does everything. Why should that distress us?

Feeling and Discernment

If feelings are so important, should we rather train people to be aware of their feelings rather than teach them discernment? The two should go together in good spiritual direction. People cannot bypass their feelings to get onto the track of discernment. Many of those repressed feelings will come up under the camouflage of consolation and desolation anyway. So in a seminar on discernment I begin by asking the people: "What are you feeling, right now?" Most of them do not even know. If we are not open with ourselves, how will we be open with God? First, we must be open to ourselves. Then we can be open to the greater depth of ourselves, which is the Spirit. Therapy and group encounters are a help for this. It would be a good way to make the examination of conscience: "What did I feel today? Was I afraid?" and so forth.

We begin this section with a famous description offered by St. Ignatius:

> [Consolation is] when an interior movement is aroused in the soul, by which it is inflamed with love of its Creator and Lord, and as a consequence, can love no creature on the face of the earth for its own sake, but only in the Creator of them all. It is likewise consolation when one sheds tears that move to the love of God, whether it be because of sorrow for sins, or because of the sufferings of Christ our Lord, or for any other reason that is immediately directed to the praise and service of God. Finally, I call consolation every increase of faith, hope, and love, and all interior joy that invites and attracts to what is heavenly and to

the salvation of one's soul by filling it with peace and quiet in its Creator and Lord. (no. 316)

CONSOLATION

We have come to the rule where Ignatius describes what consolation is. Where the evil spirit produces desolation; the good spirit produces consolation. Ignatius calls consolation "increase of faith, hope, and love," "tears," "peace," and much like a quiet attraction to heavenly things. But the most basic thing about consolation is the inability to love anything, except God in God and for God, since we are so full of love for God. This is what the Lord said: "The Lord is our God, the Lord alone! Therefore, you shall love the Lord, your God, with all your heart, and with all your soul, and with all your might" (Deuteronomy 6:4–5). This is what consolation is, an experience, not therapy. It is not something that we want to do, not a principle, but we "feel" it at different levels. We may not feel it emotionally when we go through what St. John of the Cross calls the "dark night," chiefly the dark night of the spirit. But we will feel it.

When St. John of the Cross speaks of the dark night, he is really speaking about painful consolation. Some people are under the impression that consolation is always delightful. This is not always the case. This inability to love anyone or anything but in God and for God is a purifying experience, and purification can be troublesome indeed. This is true to such an extent that, when John of the Cross speaks of the dark night of the spirit, he says that it is like the pains of hell and yet the person who is going through it does not want to be released from it, because he has a feeling of *Someone* pressing in upon him. If and when this is lifted, he has the feeling of being alone, and he does not want that. If this is what consolation is and gives us, an experience of unity with the Other, it is something to be desired, sought after, appreciated, treasured, and prayed for! This was considered very new doctrine about fifteen to twenty years ago, because we had been taught that consolation is something to which one does not pay too much attention.

Some say: "A person should be indifferent. Whether we have consolation or not, it does not matter." This is completely false, like saying whether you are detached or not does not matter. Others say: "We must love the God of all consolations, not the consolations of God." This is pure spiritual tripe. Consolation means nothing else but an intensity of love that leads to complete detachment and indifference. We cannot produce this. This is a gift given from God. That is the reason why we should be encouraged to do everything to get it. When Ignatius talks about penance, he says that one reason for doing penance is "[t]o obtain some grace or gift that one earnestly desires" (no. 87). And in his terminology *gift* or *grace* is synonymous with *consolation*. He gives examples such as weeping much over one's sins, or deep sorrow because of the sufferings of Christ. Tears are consolations. One of the reasons for doing penance is to weep much. So Ignatius wants us to seek consolation, pray for it, to make some change in the kind of penance in order to get it. For him it is obviously something to be desired.

Ignatius asks us in the *Constitutions of the Society of Jesus* to "earnestly endeavor to attain devotion in the spiritual duties." Devotion equals consolation. So one of the things we must ask ourselves after an hour of prayer is "Did I earnestly endeavor to get devotion?" Now, it is because we have neglected this that the spiritual life of so many people has suffered very much, and remained a dry kind of life. It is like two married people who decide to love one another and have no feelings whatsoever. No experience of love, just the will and principles. What kind of a life can one lead with God unless he or she experiences consolations?

Once, after listening to a tertian, I told him, "The thing you need most is to become pious once again." And he was horrified. What nonsense, I thought! We have picked up a kind of "manly" spirituality from the American cowboy or the Prussian general. This is a man? This is what we have to be in the spiritual life, nothing of soft, sentimental feelings, tears? We must be manly? We do not realize that the American cowboy is not a true man at all, but the caricature of a man, a brute. A man is human. I have already spoken highly of him, but I will do so again. For me, a man is St. Francis Xavier (1506–1552). What courage this man had, moving into new places, risking his life among the cannibals, without two revolvers on his hip to defend himself. He goes there with a cross, and he is frightened. He is tremendously brave, and then he will be crying in his prayers and full of consolation. Nobody would say that Ignatius was not a manly man, and yet he could hardly say a line of his breviary without weeping. He had an intense gift of tears. This is manly, and being human. There was a kind of revulsion against feelings in our spiritual life. But we are outgrowing that very fast, and consolation is once again being prized.

The motives for this moving to the love of God and the gift of tears could be different: our sorrow for sins, the suffering of Christ, or other reasons. The motive that moved

Ignatius most was the contemplation of the three divine persons. Whatever the motive, the tears always cause an increase in the love of God. The basic thing in consolation is an increase in love, hope, faith, interior joy, an attraction to heavenly things, and peace.

Before we move on, we have to distinguish between two types of consolation: (1) *sensible* consolation, referring to the senses; and (2) *spiritual* consolation, which cannot be perceived so directly by the senses or with the body. It is not so much an emotion. *Sensible consolation* is the kind of consolation we have traditionally associated with novices. For them there is a novelty in the spiritual life, everything is so new, and everything is so exciting. It is like the love of people who have just fallen in love. There is vehemence; they are full of passion, and a lot of turbulence. Give them a few months and the feelings will quiet down. Does that mean that their love has grown less? No, it has probably increased. The love is deeper, the bond has grown, but there is less feeling. The feelings may spurt up occasionally, but the intensity and the vehemence have died down. This is what happens to us with regard to God also. When we first fall in love with God, everything is so exciting, everything is so wonderful. There is a lot of sensible consolation: tears, warmth, tenderness, and devotion. But sooner or later that dies out.

But does it have to? The tragedy is that many spiritual fathers will tell us that this consolation has to go or will eventually go! That is false! This type of consolation does not have to go. Certainly feelings and experiences evolve, but we get something much nicer, something much more appetizing, and something much more fulfilling. I remember a spiritual father talking to a group of novices. They were feeling a great deal of consolation, but he told them: "Wait a while, this will go, and then you will have to come to grips with reality. God is giving you milk for little children. The time will come when he gives you the hard bread of the adult." That approach was very discouraging. They should have been told: "This vehemence will probably—not necessarily—disappear. But it will give way to something much more delightful, much more appetizing that you will enjoy much more; it will give way to *spiritual consolation*. What is this? A sense of deep peace, of deep quiet, of being rooted in God, of great strength, of a happiness that is much deeper than the vehemence you experience now."

Read St. John of the Cross on the dark night of the senses; namely, when the senses have nothing and sensible consolation has disappeared. A person in this situation goes to the chapel and feels nothing. The vehemence and devotion, tears and warmth, all dry! On the level of the senses there is dryness; we cannot think, use our minds, and work with imagery and with fantasy. Now is the time, says St. John of the Cross, to stay in a loving, dark awareness of God. What does one do there? Nothing, we are just being present to God. Just stay with it. After a while we will experience a deep peace, a quietness of heart, and a holy union. And we would not exchange that for all the consolations in the world. A person feels peaceful, quiet, and strengthened. But for this we have to develop a taste. It is an acquired taste.

I frequently give the example of beer. If we give a child beer, he does not like it. It is bitter and he does not appreciate it. Give him a soft drink and he likes it very much. But when he has grown up, he will prefer the beer. This is an acquired taste. Or what is poetry or a symphony of Beethoven to a child? Nothing. Once one acquires the taste, it is very delightful. We need to acquire a taste for spiritual consolation. And we are lucky if, at this stage of our spiritual life, we find a director who will show us how to get a taste for it. Then it is delightful and we would not exchange it for all sensible consolations. Consolation never goes away; it stays and takes on another form. If we acquire a taste for this other spiritual form, we will find it more profitable, nourishing, and even more delightful. The mystics speak of the senses and feelings being limited. They cannot penetrate too deep. So we have to go in for another experience, an experience beyond feeling that penetrates to what they call spirit.

Why does God give sensible consolation? He is weaning people away from worldly things to develop in them a spiritual taste. They are probably too drowned in the world of matter and the world of the senses. Now, if you give them something spiritual too soon, it won't have any appeal to them. This is what God does in the beginning; he gives us something that is pleasing to the senses. He starts from where we are, so that we may get the strength and courage to wean ourselves away and become more independent. All the great mystics encourage us to seek and desire this.

SPIRITUAL DESOLATION

Desolation is entirely the opposite of what is described in the third rule about consolation (no. 316). It involves, Ignatius says, "darkness of soul, turmoil of spirit, inclination to what is low and earthly, restlessness rising from many disturbances and temptations which lead to want of faith, want of hope, want of love. The soul is wholly slothful, tepid, sad, and separated, as it were, from its Creator and Lord. For just as consolation is the opposite of desolation, so the thoughts that spring from consolation are the opposite of those that spring from desolation" (no. 317). For Ignatius, *desolation* is synonymous with *temptation*. We may never desire, seek, or ask for desolation. That would be ridiculous. Obviously temptation can have good effects on a person. But we may not ask for it; it is an evil, to be avoided. God never *causes* desolations, but he does *allow* them. And we are supposed to do everything possible to get out of desolation. The most dangerous, the most subtle of all these desolations is what Ignatius calls the "inclination to what is low and earthly." The other desolations as we've already mentioned—turmoil, darkness of soul, tepidity, sadness—are quite painful, and nobody wants to stay in them. Just as consolation is attraction to heavenly things, desolation is attraction to worldly things, to the extent that the spirit in a person dies. He or she is no longer attuned to the spirit. It is as if the animal in a person has taken over.

As I already mentioned, consolation need not necessarily be delightful; it can be painful. The dark night, which can be a form of consolation, is like being hugged by someone whom we love very much. It is delightful, but extremely painful at the same time. St. John of the Cross says the grace of the dark night is exactly the same as the grace that follows it. When the darkness has lifted, we are in full brightness. The same brightness was there before, but our eyes were diseased. As our eyes become healthy, the darkness changes into light.

Desolation can also be quite pleasant and delightful. You may have a person who is getting on very well, everything is succeeding, and his or her projects are going ahead. Imag-

ine that today is a holiday and a certain person is going out
for dinner or a movie, and all is well with the world. The
individual is perfectly and blissfully happy. Then we say to
him or her, "You are in desolation."

"No, I am perfectly happy."

"Just sit down for ten minutes and pray."

And the person cannot get anywhere; he or she is dis-
gusted and will get out of the chapel. Desolation! The person is happy, all right, but not on the level of the spirit. If
this individual gets to the level of the spirit, he or she will
realize that something is wrong. There is a strong inclination to what is low and earthly. I am not saying they should
not enjoy the good things of earth, but such persons are
getting drowned in them. Where there is no spiritual appetite, there is desolation. This is the most subtle and dangerous kind of desolation. When the appetite for spiritual
things is lost, everything is lost. We will meet people who
do not have much sensible comfort in prayer, but they will
have a strong appetite for prayer and a deep appetite for
God. All is well, do not worry. Perhaps the way to discern
and judge the spiritual stage of a person is to check his or
her appetite for God, for prayer, and for the world of the
spirit. If it is there, all is right.

"In time of desolation," Ignatius advises, "we should never
make any change, but remain firm and constant in the resolution and decision which guided us the day before the
desolation, or in the decision to which we adhered in the
preceding consolation. For just as in consolation the good
spirit guides and counsels us, so in desolation the evil spirit
guides and counsels. Following his counsels we can never
find the way to a right decision" (no. 318). The key idea in
this fifth rule is "Never change in time of desolation." That is

a simple enough rule, but unfortunately it is not always observed, and so desolation creates a lot of problems for people. The same is true with a vocation problem. If one is in desolation, do not raise the question. As long as a person is in desolation, stick it out. That is not the time for change. They should do what they ordinarily are doing, or what was revealed to them in the time of a previous consolation. Do not change. Then the second thing is: "In [time of] desolation the evil spirit guides and counsels." This is important to keep in mind. Some say that desolation lasts a very long time. Desolation does not last very long. Consolation will soon return.

"Though in desolation we must never change our former resolutions, it will be very advantageous to intensify our activity against the desolation. We can insist more upon prayer, upon meditation, and on much examination of ourselves. We can make an effort in a suitable way to do some penance" (no. 319). This sixth rule is so typical of Ignatius: Do not defend; attack! When we are tempted to pray less, we should pray a little more. When we are tempted to eat more, eat a little less. Do not just defend yourself against the enemy. This advice has its value if applied with a certain amount of common sense. If we are tempted after Mass to leave after five minutes, while we had originally planned to stay for ten, we should stay for twelve minutes. What is the advantage of this? It is psychological: We know now that in the future it is useless to be tempted, because we gave ourselves more time. So it is less likely we will be tempted again. This, however, can be overdone, so we must remain diligent.

Frequently the desolations people have are not desolations at all; they are depressions. They are sick and tired of prayer and the spiritual life in the way that they are sick and tired of their best friend. They will be sick and tired of the Lord also. So they need to take a holiday from the Lord. Let them go, enjoy themselves, have a good time, and come back. And then they will be ready for him again, and ready for the spiritual life once more. A Chinese proverb says: "If you stretch the bow too much, you will regret it." I like what they said about the foundress of the Maryknoll Sisters: "She was a woman who had a cool head, a warm heart, and a sense of humor." That is what we need: a warm heart, ready to go all out with total generosity and greatheartedness; a cool head to be used for calculating how much we can do; and then a sense of humor. Sit lightly on everything. Do not take anything too seriously, God included. G. K. Chesterton (1874–1936) said: "There is nothing so sacred that you cannot make a joke out of it." So let us not take ourselves or anything else too seriously.

If someone is in desolation, we might send him to pray more. Or does he just need a little break? If the desolation includes a loss of appetite for God and prayer, it may be good to apply what Ignatius says about penance in no. 319. Penance is not unpleasant, if we know how to practice it. Fasting is not an unpleasant, but a delightful, exercise, if we know how to practice it. If we find penance unpleasant, then we have to learn how to practice it the right way. Ignatius was a great believer in the use of penance to overcome the attacks of the devil and temptations, and to bring about consolations.

Ignatius speaks about intensifying our activity against desolation. So desolation is something we must fight. When people are going through some prolonged desolation because of their negligence and tepidity, when they feel a lack of appetite in the spiritual life and a disgust for the spiritual things, and when there is a sense of "I don't believe any longer, the spiritual life means nothing to me," then that is a real crisis situation. Now this person must get into prayer. The longer this situation lasts, the more the acid keeps eating into people, and the greater the harm done. They must find periods of silence, periods when they can get away and be with themselves. That is the time when we indulge all kinds of rationalizations such as "Prayer is not my way." We will find a lot of excuses. The human mind is the slave of the heart. When people do not want things, they can get their mind to produce all kinds of reasons.

A good example is Jesus himself. When he was in desolation, he took himself to prayer. And it is interesting to see the kind of prayer he used: petitionary and ejaculatory prayer. "My Father, if it is possible, let this cup pass from me; yet not what I want but what you want" (Matt. 26:3), and he repeated this again and again. After a while he was consoled. He was more in possession of himself and consoled by God. This is what people in desolation must be encouraged to do.

In a seventh rule Ignatius gives this advice: "When one is in desolation, he should be mindful that God has left him to his natural powers to resist the different agitations and temptations of the enemy in order to try him. He can resist with the help of God, which always remains, though he may not clearly perceive it. For though God has taken from him the abundance of fervor and overflowing love and the intensity of his favors, nevertheless, he has sufficient grace for eternal salvation" (no. 320).

We are never so abandoned that we do not have help from God, even though we may not clearly perceive this. A person can find consolation in the conviction: "For though

God has taken from him the abundance of fervor and over-flowing love and the intensity of his favors, nevertheless, he has sufficient grace for eternal salvation." Notice, God has not taken away fervor, but the abundance of fervor. He has not taken away love, because that always remains; the over-flowing love and the intensity of favors have been removed. For Ignatius, a person who has given his or her life to God and is serving him with good will and generosity will almost invariably have devotion. There will always be some mea-sure of devotion. The coal will be glowing there, covered with ashes—the embers are always glowing. The spiritual person is never without consolation; there is always some. That is why Ignatius tells us to seek devotion and ask our-selves after prayer, "Did I have the feeling of devotion?"

"When one is in desolation, he should strive to persevere in patience. This reacts against the vexations that have overtaken him. Let him consider, too, that consolation will soon return, and in the meantime, he must diligently use the means against desolation" (no. 321). In this eighth rule Ig-natius in effect says to us: "Do not be anxious; all is well. Do not be worried; this is part of our growth. Have patience." If we are patient with ourselves and look kindly upon ourselves, that is one of the effective ways to overcome desolation.

REASONS FOR DESOLATION

Ignatius explains in a ninth rule the reasons why desola-tions occur:

> The principal reasons why we suffer from desolation
> are three:

The first is because we have been tepid and slothful or negligent in our exercises of piety, and so through our own fault spiritual consolation has been taken away from us.

The second reason is because God wishes to try us, to see how much we are worth, and how much we will advance in his service and praise when left without the generous reward of consolations and signal favors.

The third reason is because God wishes to give us a true knowledge and understanding of ourselves, so that we may have an intimate perception of the fact that it is not within our power to acquire and attain great devotion, intense love, tears, or any other spiritual consolation; but that all this is the gift and grace of God our Lord. God does not wish us to build on the property of another, to rise up in spirit in a certain pride and vainglory and attribute to ourselves the devotion and other effects of spiritual consolation. (no. 322)

When desolation comes, the first thing to ask ourselves is: Have I been lazy, negligent, or slothful? Desolation may be God's way of saying that we are not eager enough. So when he withdraws consolation, we seek him and become more diligent. St. Bernard says that when the bridegroom goes away, he starts crying out for him. We see that we can do nothing without him. God wants to give us true knowledge about ourselves, "so that we may have an intimate perception of the fact that it is not within our power to acquire and attain great devotion, intense love, tears, or any other spiritual consolation; but that all this is the gift and grace of God our Lord."

José Calveras maintains that it is not possible to make the Exercises without experiencing mystical graces, graces that we cannot produce by ourselves. God gives them and God wants us to have an intimate perception of the fact that they come from him. So one day we are swimming in consolation, we are delighted, and convinced that now we have made it. We have entered into the grace stream, the great river that leads down to the ocean, and we will merge with the Infinite. The next day we are dry, hard, and just our old self. And there is nothing we can do to bring back the experience of the previous day. God wants us to realize that we constantly depend on him: "[A]part from me you can do nothing" (John 15:5). Petitionary prayer and a sense of our helplessness and need will bring back consolation. "God does not wish us to build on the property of another, to rise up in spirit in a certain pride and vainglory and attribute to ourselves the devotion and other effects of spiritual consolation." The worst thing that could happen to us would be that we become like Lucifer, who attributed to himself his spiritual graces. In practice this is not too much of a problem, but one never knows. Ignatius himself was very leery of people given to prayer, because they tended to become very proud and defensive. They were no longer open. This is one of the hazards of holiness. We become convinced that we have a direct line to the Holy Spirit. God frequently removes this line, so that we may realize that we are helpless and need him.

The tenth rule states: "When one enjoys consolation, let him consider how he will conduct himself during the time of ensuing desolation, and store up a supply of strength as defense against that day" (no. 323). This rule is frequently misinterpreted to mean: If we are in consolation, remember that desolation will come. Ruin the picnic! It is not that at all. Ignatius says: When we are in consolation, now is the time to make plans. What are we going to do and how are we going to act when the next desolation comes? Now we are united with God. Now is the time to make decisions and find out his will. "Store up a supply of strength" means "Give in to it, enjoy it. Surrender to the grace, enjoy your picnic."

As Ignatius says in the Jesuit *Constitutions*: "Let them all advance in true virtue, whether with more visitations [consolations] or fewer." He does not say "visitations or no visitations," but "more [consolations] or fewer," because we always need consolation in order to advance in true and solid spiritual virtue. It is not possible to advance in virtue without consolation. As Ignatius wrote to St. Francis Borgia: "[W]ithout these consolations all our thoughts, words, and actions are tainted, cold, and disordered." Teresa of Avila used the metaphor of water. "You want to grow flowers of virtues in the garden of your heart. You have to water the plants." Water stands for the graces and devotion. There are four ways she describes for getting water. One is by drawing it from the well; another is by means of a water wheel and aqueducts; a third way is to get it from a river or stream, and the water comes in without any effort; and finally water may arrive from heaven when it rains. She wrote: "I cannot believe that anyone, who really attempts to, will not get all of these graces. Mystical graces are for everyone. You need the water of devotion and consolation for the virtues to grow." This makes good sense even psychologically. What kind of virtue is it if it is only willpower? It is not spontaneous or natural. When our heart is aflame with the felt love for God, virtues flow spontaneously.

Ignatius adds further advice in the eleventh rule:

> He who enjoys consolation should take care to humble himself and lower himself as much as possible. Let him recall how little he is able to do in time of desolation, when he is left without such grace or consolation.
>
> On the other hand, one who suffers desolation should remember that by making use of the sufficient grace offered him, he can do much to withstand all his enemies. Let him find his strength in his Creator and Lord. (no. 324)

Here let me make only one comment. If consolation comes from God, we do not have to go out of our way to humble ourselves, because we will automatically feel very humble. We will not even be tempted to become proud.

When desolation comes, Ignatius recommends three things. First, a twelfth rule: Do not be scared or frightened (no. 325). Second, be transparent and disclose to some spiritual person the devil's "evil suggestions" (no. 326). Openness is a great help. St. Thérèse of the Child Jesus (1873–1897) writes of being liberated from a temptation by simply going and speaking to someone about it. She felt very shy and embarrassed, but went and spoke of the temptation and it disappeared. Sometimes we notice this with retreatants. As soon as they describe their desolation to us, it goes away. This can be explained psychologically, too. Once we explain our distress, we feel relieved.

Thirdly, Ignatius introduces a military analogy:

> The conduct of our enemy may also be compared to the tactics of a leader intent upon seizing and plundering a position he desires. A commander and leader

of an army will encamp, explore the fortifications and defenses of the stronghold, and attack at the weakest point. In the same way, the enemy of our human nature investigates from every side all our virtues . . . Where he finds the defenses of eternal salvation weakest and most deficient, there he attacks and tries to take us by storm. (no. 327)

This final recommendation calls for vigilance. Be on alert, be aware of what is going on, be attuned to the movements of these spirits. The price of freedom is eternal vigilance.

FURTHER RULES

Ignatius moves on to a further set of rules for "discernment of spirits." At the start he told us that desolation is caused by the evil spirit and consolation by the good spirit. Now he says consolation can be caused by the good or evil spirit, and we have to be more wary. There is nothing, it seems, produced by God that cannot be counterfeited by the evil spirit. In other words, there is no good thing that cannot become bad, just as there is no bad thing that cannot be made into good. To help us discern the difference, Ignatius declares:

It is characteristic of God and his angels, when they act upon the soul, to give true happiness and spiritual joy, and to banish all the sadness and disturbances which are caused by the enemy.

It is characteristic of the evil one to fight against such happiness and consolation by proposing falla-

cious reasonings, subtleties, and continual deceptions.
(no. 329)

Let's talk quickly again about fallacious reasoning. Here
are two examples. Someone can say: "Look at my community. Everything is going to the dogs; nothing is being done.
The Church is going to the dogs; that's a calamity." Some
may be thoroughly distressed and upset that we have two
calamities on our hands. Another person can say the same
thing and be filled with enthusiasm: "Let us do something
about it, but we will be patient and bide our time." But the
first guy feels that he is a prophet, that he has to do something at once; he gets all bitter and upset. We can begin to
mistrust his prophetic mission. Prophets are never bitter.
One of the nicest things about Pierre Teilhard de Chardin
is that we cannot find a single bitter line in anything he
wrote. And he had cause for bitterness! He would be deeply
grieved, in tears, crushed, but never bitter. When we are all
upset, bitter, and angry, we can ask ourselves whether it is
really the good spirit leading us. This does not mean we have
to be fools. We can see all that is wrong, but when we are
under the influence of the good spirit, we act in one way;
when under the influence of the evil spirit, we see the same
thing and we act in another way.

Some people ask the question: "Are these spirits real entities? Are they personalities?" We could discuss this forever
and ever. We might reply, "This man is moved by a spirit of
vanity, a spirit of charity, a spirit of abnegation," and we are
not talking about personal entities. We see the movement
of spirits and their effects. Whether or not some movement
is literally caused by Lucifer, we need not bother.

At this point Ignatius adds a famous observation about

consolation: "God alone can give consolation to the soul without any previous cause. It belongs solely to the Creator to come into a soul, to leave it, to act upon it, to draw it wholly to the love of his Divine Majesty. I said without previous cause, that is, without any preceding perception or knowledge of any subject by which a soul might be led to such a consolation through its own acts of intellect and will" (no. 330). Ignatius is aware that there are moments in our lives when we experience an intense consolation and something is revealed to us. This thing happens: A course of action is proposed to us, and we cannot resist. We just follow, no matter what anybody says.

This takes us to rule eight and a qualification. Ignatius adds:

> When consolation is without previous cause, as was said, there can be no deception in it, since it can proceed from God our Lord only. But a spiritual person who has received such a consolation must consider it very attentively, and must cautiously distinguish the actual time of the consolation from the period which follows it. At such a time the soul is still fervent and favored with the grace and aftereffects of the consolation which has passed. In this second period the soul frequently forms various resolutions and plans which are not granted directly by God our Lord. They may come from our own reasoning on the relations of our concepts and on the consequences of our judgments, or they may come from the good or evil spirit. Hence, they must be carefully examined before they are given full approval and put into execution. (no. 336)

It can happen where there is no possibility of deception; we just follow no matter what anybody on this earth says. But we have to make sure that the consolation is without a preceding cause. How do we do that? Well, a preceding cause for Ignatius would be the case of a person meditating on something pious, thinking of something very holy, and then being able to explain how this consolation came. The consolation comes through the person's thoughts, images, and fantasies. They have caused the consolation. Even though the fantasy and the thoughts are not in proportion to the consolation, there is some [human] cause. What Ignatius is talking about is a time when there is no [created] cause. He bases himself on the doctrine of the scholastics that the spirits, good and evil, the angels and the devils, cannot act upon our spirits except through images and phantasms [mental forms]. So they will use images to act on us. If there is an action in the core or center of our being without phantasms being involved, they say it is only God who can do that. This view, that God can move right into the heart of our spirit, is based on the philosophy and theology of St. Thomas Aquinas.

What about the spiritual person who has received such a consolation? For instance, at ten o'clock in the morning, I suddenly experience an intense consolation. I bend down to tie my shoelaces and I am flooded with consolation. It is revealed to me that I must spend seven hours a day in prayer. I cannot doubt it; it just hits me all of a sudden. Now this lasts from 10:00 till 10:10. Then the intensity disappears. I am all aglow and I say: "What shall I do for the Lord? I shall be most generous; I will make it nine hours." Wait, wait, the other two hours came from me. The addition of two hours may be good, it may be bad. We have to examine that on the basis of other rules. But the seven hours, we know we have to do, and if we do not, we will know that we are fooling ourselves. We will know as long as we are alive what was revealed to us at that time, and that we were not faithful. Such things happen. This is the only way we can explain how the great saints were perfectly irrational. They did things against all prudence, common sense, and still they knew these things had to be done. They might start an enterprise that cost $50 million, and they did not even have a cent in their pockets. Now back to two previous ideas.

Ignatius writes: "If a cause precedes, both the good angel and the evil spirit can give consolation to a soul, but for a quite different purpose. The good angel consoles for the progress of the soul, that it may advance and rise to what is more perfect. The evil spirit consoles for purposes that are the contrary, and that afterwards he might draw the soul to his own perverse intentions and wickedness" (no. 331).

He then goes on to say: "It is a mark of the evil spirit to assume the appearance of an angel of light [2 Cor. 11:14]. He begins by suggesting thoughts that are suited to a devout soul, and ends by suggesting his own. For example, he will suggest holy and pious thoughts that are wholly in conformity with the sanctity of the soul. Afterwards, he will endeavor little by little to end by drawing the soul into his hidden snares and evil designs" (no. 332).

The evil spirit will not start tempting you with something that is openly wicked. He will say: "You are holy; you want to do great things for God. And you have to show your love for God through love for neighbor. Look at the poor people around. Do something for them, get started." So we get started on something that is holy and good, and it will not be very long before we ask: Where are we going?

That is where Ignatius says: "Caution!" How do we detect a consolation from the evil spirit? The evil spirit has to cover himself up as an angel of light.

Father Maurice Giuliani has a very nice synthesis of this. He says that in the face of a great inspiration the soul passes through four stages. (1) The good spirit does this: first, confusion and humility. "Lord I am not worthy." It is thus that all great works begin (for instance, with Moses, Isaiah, Our Lady, Peter, all of them). They are suddenly confronted with the divine and their first response is one of unworthiness: "Will I really measure up? I am so inadequate." God consoles them with his power and grace. (2) The next step is the surrender of the heart that is completely disinterested. (3) The third step is charity. One gets to work with great devotedness. (4) And finally: peace in action. To summarize, we start with humility and confusion, we move to surrender of oneself, then on to great devotedness and charity, and then comes peace in action.

With the evil spirit it is the contrary. One begins with charity, or what one believes to be charity. Second: there is trouble when faced with an obstacle that presents itself, or what today we call frustration. Have you ever heard of a saint who was frustrated? Saints and animals never get frustrated; they go at it again and again. Frustration is an interesting phenomenon to examine. Third: sadness, discouragement, and despondency. And finally: total inertia and maybe bitterness. And then we become cynical.

Ignatius urges us to weigh up what is happening within us:

> We must carefully observe the whole course of our
> thoughts. If the beginning, middle, and end of the
> course of thoughts are wholly good and directed to

what is entirely right, it is a sign that they are from the good angel. But the course of thoughts suggested to us may terminate in something evil, or distracting, or less good than the soul had formerly proposed to do. Again, it may end in what weakens the soul, or disquiets it; or by destroying the peace, tranquillity, and quiet which it had before, it may cause disturbance to the soul. These things are a clear sign that the thoughts are proceeding from the evil spirit, the enemy of our progress and eternal salvation. (no. 333)

Ignatius urges us to review carefully what happens.

When the enemy of our human nature has been detected and recognized by the trail of evil marking his course and by the wicked end to which he leads us, it will be profitable for one who has been tempted to review immediately the whole course of the temptation. Let him consider the series of good thoughts, how they arose, how the evil one gradually attempted to make him step down from the state of spiritual delight and joy in which he was, till finally he drew him to his wicked designs. The purpose of this review is that once such an experience has been understood and carefully observed, we may guard ourselves for the future against the customary deceits of the enemy. (no. 334)

Inevitably we detect the evil one when spiritual delight and joy begin to vanish. They become less and less, and we say: "Something is wrong here." We must examine ourselves again and again, and we will develop a sense of what is a good consolation, a real consolation that brings great peace and humility, and what is only an apparent consolation, one that brings uneasiness and stirs us up. Ignatius remarks on the difference between the two.

> In souls that are progressing to greater perfection, the action of the good angel is delicate, gentle, delightful. It may be compared to a drop of water penetrating a sponge.
>
> The action of the evil spirit upon such souls is violent, noisy, and disturbing. It may be compared to a drop of water falling upon a stone.
>
> In souls that are going from bad to worse, the action of the spirits mentioned above is just the reverse. The reason for this is to be sought in the opposition or similarity of these souls to the different kinds of spirits. When the disposition is contrary to that of the spirits, they enter with noise and commotion that are easily perceived. When the disposition is similar to that of the spirits, they enter silently, as one coming into his own house when the doors are open. (no. 335)

Giuliani again has another fine synthesis. He says that we are constantly under the influence of the spirits. In all the movements of the day we are being solicited by two camps. More and more one clearly sees if one obeys this spirit or that, if one is faithful or not. The whole of the interior life consists above all in this fidelity to interior inspirations. "Where is God leading me now? What does he want me to do now? Where is he pushing me? From where is he holding me back?" When there are no movements, it is necessary to ask: "What is lacking? Not enough prayer, not enough humility, etc.?" The tactics of the spirits are as follows: The Holy Spirit brings measure, balance, clarity, and transparency. The evil spirit brings excess and obscurity. I cannot speak; I cannot express what is going on. Finally, the Holy Spirit brings peace while the evil one brings trouble. Giuliani says very nicely that the balance of the Holy Spirit is not the middle of the road, but in keeping both extremes. The evil spirit keeps only one extreme.

One day I put down as many examples as I could think of to illustrate this point and I would like to share them with you.

One, we have total love for creatures, and total detachment from all creatures. This is the kind of balance that the Holy Spirit gives. The evil spirit gives us one or the other: a person who is totally detached and does not care about anyone, or a person who is totally attached and has no freedom whatsoever.

Two, another pair of "extremes" is "a sense of personal worth and deep humility." This is the attitude of "everything matters." This attitude entails total commitment to the progress of humanity, social involvement, and a sense that everything matters, and, at the same time, a sense that nothing really matters. There is a deep peace in our heart when we are in touch with the Absolute and we can see the world for what it really is. Teilhard would say: "You need a new saint who is at once more detached than any of the saints of the past, and more involved than any of the saints of the past." This attitude combines total disinterest and a tremendous appetite for life.

Three, another way to express the extremes would be awareness of our sinfulness and of our lovableness.

Four, we can also think of one who has total peace of heart, and is also a spiritual warrior.

Five, Jesus spoke of being shrewd as serpents and simple as doves. Such persons trust others and at the same time know what is in their heart.

Six, Tukaram says, "We disciples of Vishnu are as soft as wax and harder than diamonds, more affectionate than a mother, and more ferocious than any enemy."

The mystics will talk about active stillness, glowing darkness, and learned ignorance. This is the kind of balance the Holy Spirit gives. If we discern the spirits for people, we must look for this balance.

8

The Third and Fourth Weeks

*I will ask for the grace to be glad and rejoice ·
intensely because of the great joy and the
glory of Christ our Lord.*
—IGNATIUS LOYOLA

*After reflecting on profound freedom ("unselfing the self"),
de Mello shows how prayer brings us to encounter the
Crucified Christ (in the "third week" of the Exercises) and
the Risen Christ (in the "fourth week").*

"The Three Degrees of Humility" could be called the high
point of the second week. In our search for God's will, we
have come to the point where we are so much in love with
Christ, and have so much indifference, that it comes to
total, complete indifference. We are so much in love with
God that we are open to health or sickness, life or death,
poverty or riches. Now this is supposed to be very intense
love for God. However, this is not the highest point in the
Exercises; the third degree of humility is something much
deeper and greater than this. We can travel much further
than this, and that is what comes in the third and fourth
weeks. The problem is really the problem of the self that I
am busy protecting. All my fears come from concerns about
the self; all my thrills come from catering to the self. How

can I become "unselfed" from the self, so that I attain total freedom?

UNSELFING THE SELF

This was something that Ramanarshi attained when he was nineteen. His whole transformation took place in one moment; he never went beyond that and it all came in that single moment. He got a tremendous fright and thought he was going to die at that moment. When the fright went away, he lay on the floor and imagined he was really dead, and in that moment he got all his mystical insights. He got "unselfed"; he saw the self for what it really was, and then he attained total and lasting peace. He certainly seems to have been an extraordinary person. Many people reported that simply sitting in his presence, he would give the *diksha*, or initiation, to people, simply by looking at them. He would let his eyes wander around the whole crowd and pick up one individual, and the person would be changed, by look or touch. This is traditional Hindu *diksha*, mere touch or look, though he would do it generally through look. He would encourage people to ask themselves continually: "Who hears? Who speaks? Constantly? After you speak, who speaks? I—who is the I? When you look, who is looking?"

This is very reminiscent of the Zen masters who would tell some of their disciples to ask themselves twenty-four hours a day: "Who am I? What am I?" And suddenly they would break, through an illumination, into the "I"; no one sees that "I" directly. When you see it directly, the implication is that there is no "I." There is an "I" but it is not the "I"; it is another "I." What is the "I"? Get in touch with it.

The fruit of unselfing the self is similar. The self is gone, but to all appearance it is exactly the same: The human being who has reached illumination talks like anybody else and acts like everybody else; there is no difference whatsoever. But the self is gone; one person has attained the *diksha*, the other has not. There is a comparison the mystics give us: We plunge into life completely, and yet we have the sense that this empirical life, the life of the senses, everything that comes to awareness, is not real. The reality is underneath, undergirding everything.

St. Teresa of Avila seems to have had this experience toward the end of her life. She said she could see herself as though she were seeing someone else. She could be totally objective about herself, as objective about herself and as concerned about herself as she was with anybody else; the selfish element of the attachment to the self was gone. Every great master has his or her own tactic for reaching this, but Teresa does not offer any tactic. The Zen masters, Ramanarshi, the Vipassana people would say: "Get in touch with your bodily sensations, and become aware of vibrations till the whole body is a mass of vibrations. When you break through to the inside, there, there is no 'I,' just vibrations. Then you are liberated. When you come to that bottom, you realize there is only 'is.' Then you are full of happiness, peace, and joy, and have nothing to protect. As long as you have an 'I' to protect and interests to look after, then you are in trouble and are never completely and totally at peace."

The strange thing about unselfing the self is this: The more we try to kill the empirical self, the more it grows, because our actions are still centered on the empirical self. We might say: "This self of mine is causing all the trouble, and that is why I am all involved, and that is the reason that I am full of distress, anxiety, and fears. Let me do something about it. I'll kill it; I'll mortify it." The more we do that, however, the more the self will grow, because the more we are mortifying it, the more we are aware of it. We do not kill it by attacking it directly. As long as it is the focus of attention, we will get nowhere. What we need is the state of thoughtlessness, the state of illumination, or the state of love where we melt into another. Most Christian mystics use this means, the loss of oneself in another. That is what Ignatius says, and what his tactic is. The last paragraph of the last instruction of the second week is "Let him desire and seek nothing except the greater praise and glory of God Our Lord as the aim of all he does. For everyone must keep in mind that in all that concerns the spiritual life his progress will be in proportion to his surrender of self-love and of his own will and interests" (no. 189).

How do we measure our progress in the spiritual life? The more we get out of our self-love, self-will, and self-interest, the more we progress. Unself the self. "For everyone must keep in mind that in all that concerns the spiritual life his progress will be in proportion to his surrender of self-love and of his own will and interests" (no. 189). These are the last lines of the second week, but they set a beautiful introduction for the third and the fourth weeks. Does this really happen with most people? No, but that is what we wish to attain. Look at how Ignatius brings this about. In the petitions of the second week: that I ask for the grace to know Christ, to love him, and to follow him. But he is distinct from me. Look, there is Christ. I want to know him, I want to love him, and I want to follow him. He is my Master, he is the Lord, and he is the General who moves ahead. Then given a choice of two things, I will choose what is more like what he chose. Now, if we look at the petitions and the fruits of the third and fourth weeks, something mysterious happens.

We are told something else in the third week: "This is to ask for what I desire. In the Passion it is proper to ask for sorrow with Christ in sorrow, anguish with Christ in anguish, tears and deep grief because of the great affliction Christ endures for me" (no. 203). Then look at the petitions of the fourth week: "Here it will be to ask for the grace to be glad and to rejoice intensely because of the great joy and glory of Christ Our Lord" (no. 221). These are all emotions. Christ is suffering? I want to suffer with him; I want to see his sufferings as mine. I want to vibrate in unison with him. If I see him glad and rejoicing, I want to feel the same joy and gladness. This is what happens when we identify with another person. The more we identify with another person, the more we will vibrate with all his emotions. He is sad, we are sad; he is happy, we are happy. It is as if I stand before Christ and I ask: "Are you happy?" He says: "Intensely happy in the light and the joy of the Resurrection!" Then all my problems, thrills, and joys fade into "Is Christ happy? I am happy." *This can only happen when we have identified with him.*

In other words, as long as I have my self-love, self-will, and self-interest, can I do the will of Christ? The love, the will, and the interests of Christ might be different from mine. For instance, I want to go to Bombay but the interests of Christ demand that I stay in Pune. Then I say, "Lord, I love you so much that I will do what is more pleasing to you and I'll stay in Pune." What Ignatius is trying to bring about is rather the following. If I could mystically identify with Christ, then there are no longer two different interests, there is only one. His interest is that I stay in Pune; that is my interest too, because he and I are the same: "[I]t is no longer I who live, but it is Christ who lives in me" (see Gal. 2:20). That is what can happen on the experiential, mystical, and emotional levels. So there are no longer two interests, just one. Then we have unselfed the self.

Now, many of the mystics have this in an experiential way and in a more or less permanent way. The unselfing through *bhakti*, or through identification with the loved one, is something you see in the third week. Yet here we could still feel his sadness or his sufferings as our own from a sense of compassion. In the fourth week, however, it is impossible to feel his joy unless we have identified with him. We know a mother achieves this with her child. When we hit the child, we hit the mother. The mother immediately participates in what happens, since it is like something done to her.

Lovers, when they love, are very intense. They identify and lose themselves in each other. Now, it is impossible to lose ourselves completely in the joy of someone else unless the identification is total. It is similar to a situation when we are intensely happy and all our troubles disappear. This is not possible through mere compassion; *we must really love*.

And that is why Ignatius gives a great importance to the fourth week; it is the most important week of the Exercises and the toughest—the time when we have to invest the greatest intensity in recollection and silence. Sadly it is the time when many retreat masters start telling jokes and creating dissipation—precisely in the time when we need the greatest concentration and the most total detachment. Here is why. We "ask for the grace to be glad and rejoice *intensely* because of the great joy and the glory of Christ our Lord" (no. 221).

This grace can be attained only in an atmosphere of the total loss of the self. The retreat master should now urge the retreatant to a final effort of recollection. I know of one re-treatant who received grace in an overwhelming and lasting degree. He showed me the place where the grace really hit him. I realized something had happened to him. When I asked what it was, he said he got this intense sense of the presence of the Lord together with an intense joy. I can imagine St. Paul was a man like that, gripped by something like that. And this is what Ignatius would like the retreatant to experience.

When we come to that crowning glory of the Exercises, the "Contemplation to Attain the Love of God," there is no mention of Christ at all. That might seem strange. The iden-tification is so total now that everything is the Father. God is everything. It is as if we have become Christ and look at the whole of creation with the eyes of Christ. We are identified now with the Divinity and there is no Christ any longer. That is theologically sound. Also for Ignatius, Christ is the way and not the goal. The nicest thing we can say to Jesus Christ is not "I love you," but "Now I am learning to love *him* as a result of being identified with you." [Karl] Rahner would say that Christ was obsessed with his Father. I would agree. His great obsession is with the Father and his whole being is toward the Father. This is the aim of the third week. How can we attain that grace that St. Paul had? Through fantasy, those contemplations, and the applica-tion of the senses. These are the ways we experience Jesus' suffering and Jesus' joy as our own and identify with him— obviously through grace and consolations.

This brings up the whole problem of looking after our-selves, of having a healthy attitude toward ourselves, of lov-ing ourselves, and of praising ourselves. How does this fit in with Ignatian doctrine? Very much so; very, very much so. It seems like a paradox because we cannot forget ourselves and really liberate ourselves until our needs are first met. When we have met our needs, we can forget ourselves. For example, we may be hungry and fasting, and we cannot get the thought of food out of our head. Then we should have a good meal and we will be free from our stomach. Otherwise the stomach claims too much of our attention. There are dangers in the area of self-abnegation, self-mortification, and self-crucifixion: the more we keep depriving ourselves of food, comforts, appreciation, praise, and love, the more the baby will start howling. Feed that blinking baby, and it will go to sleep and we are freed from the baby. Then we can move on and do other things. Otherwise that baby will be howling the whole day: meet the baby's needs. Meet your needs, cater to all the reasonable needs of the self, and, having done that, push on further; there is something deeper to be found.

There is something deeper and more beautiful in human life than the base instincts of the animal level. I call this human and not supernatural. The divine, the infinite, the deeper self are all part of our humanity. Go in quest of the deeper self. Then we are ultimately liberated from the normal fears, joys, and all that we experience, because there is a deeper level that is made available to us. Some mystics have attained this deep level and have met the needs of the empirical self since that baby stopped howling. But other mystics have reached this level and the child is still yelling, and they are very poor specimens of humanity. That is a tragedy.

True spirituality would take into account the whole person. All of a person is spiritual, even when we are meeting the needs of the empirical self. The Word becomes flesh, and flesh is part of spirit—Teilhard is full of that theme. Meet the whole of flesh; do not run away from humanity to attain real spirituality. Unself the self, and notice how we are unselfing the self not out of hatred, or a desire to kill the evil self. The self has a reality of its own, a grim reality, perhaps, but one that is beautiful, charged with God's glory, and having its rights and its needs. When these needs are met, we can transcend self. We do not kill it or destroy it. Rather, having transcended it, a greater beauty comes into it. What is more beautiful than the one who has made the breakthrough to the mystical and the divine? We are not going to suffer for the sake of suffering or go to the cross simply for the sake of the cross. Crucifixion is not a value in itself. Do not try to unself the self through crucifixion; unself the self through mystical identification and love.

Scripture Texts for the Third Week

A few Scripture texts connected with the third week are helpful for retreatants; they are texts connected with that keynote of generosity in the third week. "What ought I to do for Christ and suffer for him" is one of the points Ignatius brings up in each of the meditations and contemplations. In a way it is the final answer to the colloquy of the first week, "What have I done for Christ? What am I doing for Christ? What ought I to do for Christ?" (no. 53). In the third week Ignatius adds "What [ought I] to do and suffer for him?" (no. 197). St. Paul brings this out very nicely in some passages: 2 Corinthians 5:14 ("For the love of Christ urges us on, because we are convinced that one has died for all; therefore all have died"); 1 Thessalonians 5:10 ("[Our Lord Jesus Christ] who died for us, so that whether we are awake or asleep we may live with him"); Romans 14:7

("We do not live to ourselves, and we do not die to ourselves").

These four texts in a way would be more than enough for the third week. The method of unselfing the self is not so much illumination as a complete surrender and going out into Christ, a complete identification with Christ.

INTRODUCTION TO THE FOURTH WEEK

Recognizing that this week requires the greatest recollection, let us now take into account a theological reflection on the whole matter of resurrection that is useful for the retreatants at this stage.

Resurrection is not the same as resuscitation. It is not the resuscitation of a dead person, as Jesus resuscitated Lazarus and the daughter of Jairus. Christ was not resuscitated; he was resurrected, which means he was not brought back to this life of ours; he was brought to another life, and this is important to understand. The life he is living now is not our life, not the human existence we are living. He has taken on a new life. It is a new creation, a new world in which he is living. So it is not the old man repaired, but rather a brand-new creature born. It is this resurrected life of his that we are sharing with him now.

Faith tells us that we are participating in his resurrected existence right now. It is already here now, and so Christ will tell us to follow him in suffering so that we can follow him in glory. Both things go hand in hand. This is very typical of John's Gospel in which Christ joins together his Crucifixion and Resurrection by speaking of being "lifted up from the earth" (John 12:32; see John 3:14 and John

8:28). Resurrection cannot be understood apart from the Crucifixion; Crucifixion cannot be understood apart from the Resurrection.

When we participate in the resurrected life, we experience his glory. As St. Paul says: "For just as the sufferings of Christ are abundant for us, so also our consolation is abundant through Christ" (2 Cor. 1:5). So many of the saints' experiences point to the Cross of Christ and simultaneously to his Resurrection. Another thing that appears when we participate in the Resurrection of Christ is a new creation, a newness of life, which becomes evident to people. Resurrected people, externally, seem to be exactly the same as anybody else, but there is a quality in their living that is radically different. The quality of their values, their attitudes, their living, is radically different.

Harvey Cox, who wrote *God's Revolution and Man's Responsibility*, speaks of this change. He speaks about this transformation through crucifixion, the resurrected life through crucifixion, and he puts it very well: "Walking in the newness of life means to now see the world 'crucifixionally,' to see the world as the place in which the crucifixion of Jesus goes on today, tomorrow, and every day. To identify ourselves with the death of Jesus is to move out and to participate in this continuing crucifixion. To walk in newness of life is to share in death." Walking in newness of life does not mean making merry and having fun; it means participating in the death of Jesus. When we participate in his death, mysteriously, a new life begins to shine in us.

Now what about the Lord's Supper? Again it is clear to me that when the Lord speaks of his cup, this cup of "the new covenant in my blood," he is also speaking of his death by crucifixion. This is the cup in which we are invited to share, so that when we drink of that cup what we are really doing is drinking of his Crucifixion and offering ourselves to identify with his Crucifixion. When Jesus took the bread, he broke it and said: "This is my body 'broken' for you." It is in the brokenness, the sharing of abuse and ridicule, and the experience of being despised and rejected by people that we partake in this bread.

It is a dangerous thing to participate in Holy Communion. Few speak of the dangers of the Eucharist. Yet when we eat broken bread, we are identifying with the broken body. When we participate in the Holy Eucharist, this is what we are offering ourselves for. Our vulnerability holds true for the cup as it is poured out. We allow ourselves to be broken and poured out: this is what we can learn here from those Eucharistic elements.

Resurrection comes through Crucifixion—through embracing life fully, living it totally, and identifying with life and living it in depth. Let me close these passages with quotations from Dietrich Bonhoeffer and Harvey Cox.

Bonhoeffer wrote: "Man is challenged to participate in the sufferings of God at the hands of a godless world. He must plunge himself in the life of a godless world without attempting to gloss over its ungodliness, with the veneer of religion or trying to transfigure it. To be a Christian does not mean to be religious in a particular way, to try to cultivate some particular form of asceticism."

This is very reminiscent of Paul. If you read First Corinthians and Colossians, you will see how he insists that asceticism or practices or fasting are very secondary. Bonhoeffer continues: "To be a Christian means to be a human being. It is not some religious act which makes the Christian what he or she is, but participation in the suffering of God in the life of the world. Jesus does not call us to a new religion but to life. What is the nature of that life? What is the nature of that participation in the powerlessness of God in the world?" This is what he says this life is: a person "is powerless against evil, he surrenders, he dies, he is murdered, he participated in that powerlessness of God in the world." This is life.

Cox remarked: "But there was not going to be a next time for Bonhoeffer; soon after he wrote those lines the Gestapo entered his cell and he was executed. There was never a next time, because instead of simply talking about participation in the suffering of God in the world, he participated."

We cannot close our eyes to this suffering when we enter into the fourth week. Some people might say: "Now we have meditated on the Passion, cried with Christ and wept with him. Let's forget all that and let's have a good time." That is a false move. To meditate in the fourth week is simply to meditate on the third week in depth and go more deeply into it.

We never get rid of the Cross and the Crucifixion. The whole point of the Resurrection is found precisely in the newness of life. We meditate on two sides of the same thing: tribulations with consolations, and moments of life with powerlessness and death. The two things go hand in hand. Hence, the third and the fourth weeks are not separate realities; they are two aspects of exactly the same reality. We can participate in or understand the Resurrection only if we are ready to integrate that vision of Julian of Norwich. She sees Jesus hanging right merrily upon his cross; he laughs right merrily upon his cross; laughing merrily, but on the cross laughing merrily. Paul links our death to the world and life to

God: "[I]t is no longer I who live" (death); "but it is Christ who lives in me" (life). In some passages of Paul we see how he brings it out sharply that death operates simultaneously with life; when he is being crucified and worn out, then life is shining out for him. Both life and death go together.

To participate in Christ's saving act is to participate in and experience his death and to die and live every day. When we participate in the Eucharist, we participate in Christ's death and his Resurrection—an experience for every day of our lives. To live the Crucifixion is to live crucifixionally, but joyously. If we live crucifixionally in gloom, it makes no sense. If we have lots of fun and do not live crucifixionally, that makes no sense either; that is not newness of life. We notice that crucifixion people are resurrection people. Paul was a crucifixion man as well as a resurrection man. We see his intense rejoicing in all his letters. St. Francis of Assisi was a crucifixion man—with such total detachment and a totally intense joy. St. Francis Xavier was also such a crucifixion and resurrection man.

That is why Ignatius insists on that fruit of the fourth week: intense joy and gladness in the gladness of Christ our Lord. He urges us to experience that intense joy, and he tells us to take it easy in this fourth week. If it helps us to feel this joy by using a fire in the winter or cool places in the summer, we should use them so that we rejoice in the Lord and not just have a good time. What Ignatius wants to show us is that we achieve this intense joy not only through fasting but also through the good things of this world. Through this way of acting let us see if we can identify and experience the joy of Christ.

In 1 Corinthians 4:10–13 Paul brings out this point very beautifully:

We are fools for the sake of Christ, but you are wise in Christ. We are weak, but you are strong. You are held in honor, but we in disrepute. To the present hour we are hungry and thirsty, we are poorly clothed and beaten and homeless, and we grow weary from the work of our own hands. When reviled, we bless; when persecuted, we endure; when slandered, we speak kindly. We have become like the rubbish of the world, the dregs of all things, to this very day.

Paul also writes in 2 Corinthians 4:16: "So we do not lose heart. Even though our outer nature is wasting away, our inner nature is being renewed day by day." Here we must recognize that Paul is not speaking of life after death, but of what we are experiencing right now. We might also check Colossians 3; Romans 6:3–11; and Philippians 3 for the theme of knowing Christ and experiencing the power of his resurrection.

This experience is like a transformation that comes upon people when they are no longer like others and yet completely similar to others. The problem of the resurrected person is that he or she has another set of values that makes no sense to the world. That is what happened to Jesus and his whole set of values; he was in touch with a reality with which the world was not in touch, and so he was utterly helpless in this world. The resurrected person: no one is so much at home in creation, or more homeless in the world. A person like St. Francis of Assisi was completely at home with creation, nature, and humanity, but not with the "world," in the sense Jesus uses the word: the world is his enemy ("I am not asking you to take them out of the world, but I ask you to protect them from the evil one" [John 17:15]). The resurrected person is so much at home among people and yet so homeless when faced with the attitude and values of people, the flesh, and the devil—so homeless in the midst of selfishness and worldliness.

Christ summons us to be persecuted and hated. [Georges] Bernanos said that Christ has called us to be the salt of the earth, not the honey of the earth—not honey pots that attract flies, but salt. If we rub salt in a wound, it hurts. Wherever a resurrected person goes, his presence is hurtful to a worldly person. It is like rubbing salt in a wound. It is like Jesus. As I said before, we may think Jesus came to produce peace. Quite the contrary. Jesus came to produce division.

One Anglican priest wrote very beautifully about the fact that for all its concern about the fact of the resurrection of Jesus, the Church has not been very great at showing the quality of the resurrected life. This is very well put indeed. This writer believed that the Church has been obsessed with showing the fact of Jesus' resurrection. He wished the Church would be less obsessed with the historical fact and would be more obsessed with showing forth the quality of the resurrection life. If the Church would give us a little more evidence of the quality of resurrection life, people would be more ready to believe in the fact of the Resurrection. Think of this kind of life as exemplified by Mahatma Gandhi. He was always cheerful, peaceful, even humorous and very serene, and he led a crucified existence.

The fruit of this fourth week is the encounter with the Risen Lord. I invite people to seek this grace in the fourth week. Many people who have not experienced such an encounter ask: "What does it mean?" If you have to ask, then ask for it. It is the birthright of every Christian to meet the Risen Lord sometime in his or her life. Anthony Bloom sensed the presence at the other end of the table: "Nothing I could do would make me doubt that this presence was Jesus the Risen Lord," and "since then I have never been the same person again and I have never been able to doubt it any more." He says: "My acquaintance with Christianity did not begin with the Annunciation, it began with the Resurrection. The Resurrection was not a fact of history for me, it was an experience."

So I tell the retreatants in the fourth week: "You have been so generous with the Lord all these days, you have such a deep spirit of recollection, now press for this grace, ask for it: to meet the Risen Lord and in this encounter to lose yourself in him, to fall in love with him and in this way get the fruit of this week." That is the reason why I encourage retreatants during this fourth week to maintain their recollection and to increase their effort to find God. I think many retreat masters miss the point when they make the retreatants laugh. Ignatius is very much against laughter during a retreat, and I agree with him. Laughter is a wonderful thing and a very good medicine, but during the retreat it is misplaced. Although it brings dissipation, which is excellent, there is, nevertheless, no greater enemy to concentration than a dissipated mind or a dissipated heart, and laughter dissipates. If we are laughing, we cannot concentrate. Once we begin to lose concentration in the fourth week and begin to make merry, then we have lost the most precious grace of this week.

If we understand things this way, we will really see how all the four weeks have the same fruit, yet each can be viewed in a different way. There is no substantial difference between the weeks, if we come to think of it. Total death and new life belong in every week. That is why Ignatius tells us to get all the fruit of the first week as though there were no weeks to follow. We cannot put rules on God. God can give us that total repentance in the first week, because that is what repentance is, abandoning oneself totally and turning totally to God. If we get to the stage of total repentance, we have made it. We have completed the whole retreat in the first week. I know one person at least who made the thirty-day retreat in ten days. Everything was given that retreatant right there.

In the second week we take the Sermon on the Mount and find repentance there. The third and the fourth weeks lead us to die to ourselves and live to Christ. The fruit is the same thing put in different ways and going into deeper levels. It is as if the center of gravity gets out of us and into God. In short, the fruit of these four weeks is "it is no longer I who live, but it is Christ who lives in me."

We should not attempt to produce all this for ourselves. Otherwise we will only run into difficulties. For example, we might take Jean Vanier, living with and for the mentally handicapped. We look at him and ourselves and say: "I haven't got that. What kind of inferior Christian I am!" That would be a whacking.

Let us not pain ourselves again and waste a lot of spiritual energy. The new life is a gift of God. There has to be a flowering that comes from within our very self, from deep down inside us. When we suddenly flower and bear the full fruit of what a human being really is, then we go out to another completely. If we try to produce this otherwise, we are in for trouble. Many retreatants try to get that fruit and start whacking themselves. We should not try to produce it by ourselves. Rather we must desire it and relax; the Lord will give it to us. The worst way to progress in the spiritual life is by making ourselves feel guilty. Let us ask the Lord to give us more if he wants more. Putting things another way, we might say: "They have their charism, I have mine."

No one can say which is better or which is worse. We each must do our own thing; we must listen to our inner voice and follow it. Our destiny will definitely lead us to the Crucifixion and the Resurrection. We can grow in that way, but not by tensing our psychological and spiritual muscles, because that will get us nowhere. We should rather ask for the graces of understanding and acceptance. By our asking for them, God will identify us more with his Son.

Contemplation to Attain the Love of God

Take, Lord, and receive all my liberty, my memory,
my understanding, and my entire will.
—IGNATIUS LOYOLA

At the end those who have made the Exercises should be
sufficiently purified and "unselfed" to grasp what love
involves. They can be led to become "contemplatives in
action" who find God "in all things."

It is significant that Ignatius never writes of love in the *Ex-*
ercises when he speaks of why we were created. He will not
say humanity is created to love God. He says: "Man is created to praise, reverence, and serve God" (no. 23). It is
something like what Jesus did when he was asked to teach
his disciples to pray. He did not say: "My God, I love you
with my whole heart and soul." He said: "Father in heaven,
may your name be glorified, may your kingdom come," and
so forth. Certainly, Ignatius speaks about love in the first
and second week of the *Exercises*, but, as some commentators have said, there is no word more dangerous in our vo-
cabulary than the word *love*. What is love? How do we
know that we have love? Ignatius is determined not to fall
into the trap of using the word indiscriminately until the

retreatant has really grasped the substance of love. When the retreatant is purified enough, unselfed enough, then he is ready for this doctrine of love (nos. 230–237).

LOVE

Ignatius develops his principle through two points. The first is that love ought to manifest itself in deeds rather than words (no. 230). It is important to realize that he does not say that love consists in deeds, as many people say, because love does not consist in deeds! Love manifests itself in deeds *rather than* in words. Furthermore, Ignatius does not say love manifests itself in deeds *and not in words*. In regard to the earthly love of men and women, I am not too sure that such a doctrine is correct. Frequently it gives us a greater thrill to hear loving words than to receive loving deeds. But where God is concerned, love manifests itself both in deeds and in words, but more in deeds than in words. If that is how love manifests itself, then what must love consist of?

The second point from Ignatius is that love consists in a mutual sharing of goods (no. 231). The lover gives and shares with the beloved what he or she possesses or something of what he or she has or is able to give, and vice versa. The beloved shares with the lover. Hence, if one has knowledge, that person shares it with the one who does not possess it, and likewise if one has honors or riches. Thus, one always gives to the other. From here, Ignatius proposes the "First Prelude" where he finds himself "standing in the presence of God our Lord and of his angels and saints, who intercede for me" (no. 232). This is very significant in the light of that extraordinary charism of reverence that

Ignatius had. Even in his most tender moments he speaks of God as his divine majesty.

From here we move to the "Second Prelude," where bowing we petition the King: "This is to ask for what I desire. Here it will be to ask for an intimate knowledge of the many blessings received, that filled with gratitude for all, I may in all things love and serve the Divine Majesty" (no. 233). The words echo the final fruit of the ascent to union with God as St. John of the Cross says. In one of his poems he states that "the whole of my being is so transformed into this beloved, and my whole occupation is to love and serve him in everything."

What is the meaning of "love and serve" for Ignatius? To serve God means to do God's will and nothing else, so that "every thought, word, and deed of mine will be purely directed to the greater service of God." If I have a million rupees and God is glorified by my keeping them, but more glorified by my giving them up, I give them up. If I speak, God will be glorified, but more if I keep silence; then I will keep silence. What is it that is more pleasing to God? I shall do that. This is Ignatius's ideal of service.

We could ask ourselves: is it possible to have this kind of disposition without a very intense love? In practice it is not possible, though Ignatius still conceives of that possibility. In the Constitutions, Ignatius writes: "All should have a right intention not only in their state of life, but in every detail, seeking in them solely to please the Divine Majesty for himself." This is the scope of the "Contemplation to Attain the Love of God": to please God. For which motive? For God himself, because he is beautiful and so lovely, and also for the many benefits with which he has presented us, rather than from fear of punishment or hope of rewards.

What is love? Love is sharing and giving. It is not choosing and doing, but it is like merging—something definitely more than service. And Ignatius gives us four points of how to attain this love. He proposes the following:

> [I will] recall to mind the blessings of creation and redemption, and the special favors I have received.
>
> I will ponder with great affection how much God our Lord has done for me, and how much he has given me of what he possesses, and finally, how much, as far as he can, the same Lord desires to give himself to me according to his divine decrees.
>
> Then I will reflect upon myself, and consider, according to all reason and justice, what I ought to offer the Divine Majesty, that is, all I possess and myself with it. Thus, as one would do who is moved by great feeling, I will make this offering of myself:
>
> Take, Lord, and receive all my liberty, my memory, my understanding, and my entire will, all that I have and possess. Thou hast given all to me. To thee, O Lord, I return it. All is thine, dispose of it wholly according to thy will. Give me thy love and thy grace, for this is sufficient for me. (no. 234)

Notice the affectivity in these words. "How much God our Lord has done for me, and how much he has given me." Love manifests itself in deeds and consists in sharing.

"Then I will reflect on myself" and make my offering. Some people have told me that they are afraid to make this offering. If they give all this to God, God may take it away. But this is ludicrous. What is God going to do with an idiot, if we lose our memory and understanding? This would be

the lazy person's offering. We give our abilities to God, and
God shall do what God wants. Let me illustrate by a comparison the point of giving our memory and understanding
to God.

I own a ship and I am going to take this ship over the
ocean, but now the ship no longer belongs to me because I
have given it over to somebody else, the captain. If the captain says the word, the ship will go. I am obviously going to
use my liberty, my mind, my memory, and my understanding, but now all these operations will be under another's
control. If the captain says the word, it will be done. Everything I do will be geared to the captain's service.

There is that resolution of Charles de Foucauld: to think
of Jesus, to talk of Jesus, to do nothing except in, for, and
through Jesus, and to consider anything else as a kind of rob-
bery, unless it is clearly the will of God that I give my mind
to that. Likewise for Ignatius everything is God's. There is
no self-interest, only God's interest. I hand over to God my
active faculties, which I continue to activate; otherwise it is
a lazy man's offering. "All is thine, dispose of it according to
thy will." I have given everything to God.

Now I ask something of him because this is an exercise
for attaining mutual love, the love of friendship, a spiritual
marriage so to speak, where I give myself to the beloved
and then ask the beloved to give himself to me. What do I
ask for? "Give me your love and your grace," meaning divine consolation and being inflamed with the love of God,
and as a consequence loving no creature in this world for its
own sake, but only for the Creator of them all. Ignatius is
saying: "Give me this: Give me this interior movement,
whereby I am inflamed with the love of you and as a consequence I can love no creature on this earth but only you.

Give me this grace; that's enough for me." When I have this consolation, then it is possible for me to do anything for God. It is another way of expressing what St. Augustine says: "Give me what you command and command whatever you want." Give me the strength, courage, and ability to do anything for God. This is the basic, most central aspect for the "Contemplation to Attain the Love of God."

How can we live out this life of love? Ignatius gives us the answer in the next three points. Seek God everywhere, so that the whole world becomes charged with the presence of the beloved. This is not the same as service. We are not just serving God, but rejoicing in God's presence. We are thrilled when we sense God's presence everywhere. It is a kind of romance going on besides the service. We are merging into God, and God merges into us; there is delight accompanying this. In the past we would say that love consists in deeds. We think that means we love God, but this is a very impoverishing doctrine. The whole purpose of the "Contemplation to Attain the Love of God" is to set the retreatant to experience a permanent movement of delight in the heart and thereby be aflame with the love of God.

There are different ways of making this contemplation. For a person to whom God has already given the grace of identification with Christ, this will be a kind of a mystical experience for him or her. However, the contemplation can be made by reflecting and thinking too. Next, I will refer briefly to the second, third, and fourth points, and then go on to speak of being a contemplative in action.

After he asks the retreatants to recall the blessings of creation, redemption, and the special favors they have received, Ignatius's second point is that the retreatants should reflect on how God dwells in creatures: in the elements giving them existence, in the plants giving them life, in the animals conferring upon them sensation, in man bestowing understanding. So he dwells in me and gives me being, life, sensation, intelligence; and makes a temple of me, since I am created in the likeness and image of the Divine Majesty.

Then I will reflect upon myself again in the manner stated in the first point, or in some other way that may seem better. (no. 235)

The question is: How does a person live out the doctrine of life, of love? The first consideration is to be aware of God's dwelling in everything. It is interesting how Ignatius will point to me, not so much to things. I am suffused with God's presence and charged with it. "[H]e . . . gives me being, life, sensation, intelligence; and makes a temple of me." As I said before, this is one way of living out this doctrine of love, to be in a state of constant awareness of the sense of God's presence within us. If God is constantly present to me in everything, I will be constantly present in God. Where there is love, a constant sense of presence happens.

The third point proposed by Ignatius runs as follows: "This is to consider how God works and labors for me in all creatures upon the face of the earth, that is, he conducts himself as one who labors. Thus, in the heavens, the elements, the plants, the fruits, the cattle, etc., he gives being, conserves them, confers life and sensation, etc." (no. 236). This is something unique to Ignatius. I do not know of any other mystic who would speak of God as the Laborer. The whole world consists of God's activities converging around me.

Ignatius gives as the fourth point: "This is to consider all blessings and gifts as descending from above. Thus, my limited power comes from the supreme and infinite power above, and so, too, justice, goodness, mercy, etc., descend from above as the rays of light descend from the sun, and as the waters flow from their fountains, etc." (no. 237).

The final motive for loving God: The finest and noblest motive is that God is lovely in himself. Whether God is in the whole creation or not, that is secondary. God is simply lovely in himself. Ignatius says: "This is to consider all blessings and gifts as descending from above" (no. 237). When many commentators invite you to consider all gifts and graces from above, they will speak of sunsets, mountains, flowers, the sea—all this is a pale reflection of God's infinite beauty. Instead, Ignatius says: "Thus, my limited power comes from the supreme and infinite power above." We must look at our loveliness. That is very beautiful. And so too is our justice, goodness, and beauty.

We come to the end of the retreat and Ignatius tells us to look at our loveliness, our goodness, beauty, etc. And this is just a reflection of God's goodness. It is very significant that he would choose this example, not other people, but ourselves. Most of us suffer in the spiritual life because we do not accept ourselves. Maybe this is the biggest obstacle to the spiritual life. We cannot see our own beauty or our own power unless we see it against the backdrop of God's loveliness.

A CONTEMPLATIVE IN ACTION

The fruit of the "Contemplation to Attain the Love of God" is to love and serve God in all things, says Ignatius.

Here I would like to make three distinctions and talk of three levels: to love God and to serve God in all things, this is one level; to love God and serve God in all actions, that would be another level; and to love God and serve God in apostolic action, that would be the third level.

The *first* level of love means: Go and serve God *in all things*. The formula that Ignatius uses urges us to find all things in God and to find God in all things. Here is something I picked up from Parmananda [Divarkar] that I find quite good. God is bread, God is people, God is my house, God is my parents. God takes the place of all these; I find all these in God. Ignatius says in the *Constitutions* that in Christ we find our parents and everything. We find all our things in Christ: "give me your love and your grace, this is enough for me." I find him everywhere.

The first level, loving and serving God in all things, is the height of contemplation. As we have seen, St. John of the Cross describes the high peak of contemplation where he finds God in all things. We find God not only in ourselves but also in all things, and we love and serve God in everything.

The *second* level, to love and serve God *in all actions*, describes contemplatives in action and makes us contemplatives in action. The first level is proper to the hermit: I find God in everything and everything in God. The second level means being a contemplative in action; it is typical, I would say, of the cloistered contemplative. If we read Thomas Merton, we will see how he did not find so much time for prayer in the monastery and that is how he discovered that contemplation has to be found in activity. This level of serving God is then typical, though not exclusively, of the contemplative who is called upon to sanctify the world through his or her activity and so finds God in action. In whatever action that person is doing, he or she is building up the world. The third level, which presupposes the other two, builds on this and depicts the apostles loving and serving God in apostolic activity.

Regarding the *second* level, to love and serve God in all action: Here I would like to provide an introduction and three presuppositions. Just as we eat to live, so we contemplate in order to do God's will. Contemplation is not an end in itself, but a means to surrender our whole being and activity into God. We contemplate in order to do God's will. The author of *The Cloud of Unknowing* says that after penetrating the cloud there is a stirring of love that starts gripping people and will take possession of them. Then he says that if we are supposed to speak and to do anything that any common person does and we refrain from it, then it will also strike us in our heart; we will feel a sharp pain until we do it.

On the other hand, if we are doing something that we are not supposed to do, it will also strike us. We are left with the near impossibility of doing or not doing anything except through the impulse of love. In one of the most beautiful passages of *The Cloud of Unknowing*, the author says we are so gripped by this power that it is like a conflagration that devours us. It grips us so that we are possessed. Contemplation leads to the transformation of our whole being, which influences all our actions. It is as though we are doing all our actions freely but we are not free; we are gripped.

For most people, doing God's will means much intense action. Yet God's will does not always mean action; we can do God's will while being a paralytic and surrendering to God's will. But for most people absorption into God's will means absorption into much activity, and we have to be ready for that. As I mentioned before, the God of the Bible is almost *always* encountered in a command. *Everywhere* he says: "Go, come, do, etc. Come follow me." God commands things we are supposed to do, and indicates responsibilities we have to take on. We rarely find anyone encountering God by squatting and contemplating; God appears and gets us moving. Of course, Jesus went to the desert, and Paul also: The Bible makes room for contemplation. But it is significant how much stress is laid on activity.

Now action can be a total escape *from* oneself. The more we plunge into activity, the less we have to confront ourselves. Yet action can also lead to the total escape *of* the self; it depends on how we perform the action. Remember the empirical self I was speaking about, the self we try to protect and so on. We can use action to defend it, to protect it, and to escape from deeper issues within ourselves. Or we can use action and wear the self out, just as we can use contemplation to wear it out. When action becomes the attrition of the illusionary self, then all action becomes contemplation, all work becomes worship, and all service of others becomes an adoration of God.

Further on we shall see what Ignatius's doctrine is: "Don't pray, act." Make action a prayer. But how will that action become a prayer? If the self has died in that action, it has become a prayer. It has become the purest prayer. So we must act, but as with *nishkam karma*, "selfless action": with no desire of fruits whatsoever for the self and simply with action for the sake of action. When the self has died our activity is ablaze with contemplation. Ignatius and others will say that we will experience more devotion when we are acting like this than when we are praying in the chapel. We will experience devotion when the self has died.

Now what is this experience and how can we attain it? I suppose we need to grasp the idea that most of us have to find God in action.

Let me give *three presuppositions* before answering. The *first* presupposition: We are not sanctified apart from action but through action. Dag Hammarskjöld (1905–1961) put it very well: "In our era the path to holiness necessarily passes through the world of action." He expressed this very beautifully in his own life.

Secondly, to attain this holiness through action we need a heart that is purified from selfishness—not totally purified from selfishness, but basically purified from selfishness. Ignatius said to Pedro de Ribadeneira that at the beginning of the spiritual life we need to give much time to prayer. This is so that the passions will die and we can unself the self. In other words, selfishness is removed once the self dies. Then, Ignatius said, we will find God in five minutes and do not need to put in hours of prayer to find God.

Then comes the *third presupposition*: when contemplation and action do not go together, then contemplation prevails over action. According to Ignatius, if people's speculation comes in the way of their union with God, they should stop the speculation; if their ministry gets in the way of their union with God, they should stop the ministry.

There was no doubt in his mind that what comes first is union with God. In fact, this is the way to pose the problem. The problem is not action or contemplation; the problem is union with God. It may even be that we are praying and we are not united with God. That is not prayer; we must get out of the chapel. It may be that we are acting very intensely and we are united with God; that is prayer.

If we are making no progress in union with God, then we should cut our ministry out, no matter whether one is the principal of a school or anything else. This is not easy, but our primary task is to be united with God, not to be a principal of a school. I know many provincials who, if someone is in a vocation crisis, are ready to do anything to help him. However, what about a person who is not having a vocation crisis, but a holiness crisis? We must be holy where we are!

FINDING GOD IN ALL THINGS

We have seen the distinction between the three levels, (1) loving and serving God in all things, (2) loving and serving God in all actions, and (3) loving and serving God in apostolic action. Now, let us take at look at Ignatius's formula for "finding God in all things."

In answering a question about the matter of the meditation most suited to the vocation of scholastics, Ignatius wrote: "The aim of their studies prevents the scholastics from making long meditations. Besides the Exercises they have one hour of prayer, etc.; they can exercise themselves in seeking the presence of Our Lord in all things, for example, in conversing with someone, in walking, looking, tasting, understanding, and in everything that we do, for it is true that his Divine Majesty is in all these things in his power and essence." Notice that in talking about finding God in all things, he spoke about seeking the presence of Our Lord "in everything we do." While all these functions are going on, we sense the presence of the Lord. Ignatius added: "And this manner of meditation, namely, finding

Our Lord and God in everything, is easier than raising ourselves to more abstract divine things, making ourselves present to them with much labor; and if we dispose ourselves, this exercise will cause great visitations from the Lord even though the time given for prayer is very brief." This was the meaning of the formula he would use: "Seek the presence of the Lord in all things. Here already you have some indication of how to get this, how to serve and love God in everything, start searching for him, searching for his presence in all your actions, in all your activity."

"Finding God in all things"—what does the expression mean? There is a very famous passage of Jerome Nadal (1507–1580) in which he explains what he means by "contemplative in action"—a phrase that Nadal coined. He writes: "What does it mean to find God in all things? Is it simply to do the will of God?" He continues: "In these ministries we must find God through peace, quiet, and the application of the inner man with light and joy and contentment and thus do we seek for the same thing in all our ministries, even the exterior ones." In another document Nadal says: "So briefly, in all our works we must find peace and quiet and devotion, since all these works must be directed to the fervor and charity and zeal for souls which must not be lost, and thus it is that we find God in everything and this is our method of prayer." What is Nadal saying? He is simply describing consolation: peace, quiet, and devotion.

In all actions, in all conversations, Ignatius felt the presence of God and contemplated the presence of God. He enjoyed that mysterious gift of seeing God. So we are entitled to be called contemplatives in action if in all things and all actions we feel the presence of God and contemplate the presence of God. We can see that this is not the same as doing the will of God in everything. To find God, to see God in all things, or to be a contemplative in action means much more than doing God's will in everything. To *feel* and *contemplate* his presence is the experience of devotion, peace, quiet, and consolation. That is why Ignatius says "contemplation to attain love of God," not "contemplation for attaining service."

Now we need to understand what all of this means. In practice it is impossible, it seems to me, to experience devotion in action—since there is no warmth without friction—unless we are really doing "the actions of a dead man" with constant abnegation and mortification. Previously, I pointed out that people who are really dead to themselves, who are doing the will of the Lord constantly, have hearts that are ablaze. So doing the will of God is obviously linked with this.

How do we attain this grace of finding God in all things? In all the documents I have read there is a key word: *solely*, *only*, or *entirely*. That is the key word—doing it *only* for God. This is the *nishkam karma*. On the day we are given the grace of doing action for the sake of action and nothing else, then our hearts will be aglow. The idea is doing action without desire for any fruit, and without any selfish intention at all. The action is done only for God's glory.

The Zen masters speak of action for the sake of action, and people object and argue that then we would have no enthusiasm. But the masters say that this is not true; the only reason we become tense and we do not plunge wholly into motion is because there is some self-seeking. When we eat solely for the action of eating, we seek nothing in it.

According to these masters we can plunge in totally and experience liberation. They are using different terms, but they are saying the same thing: doing things solely for God. How do we attain this? People suggest all sorts of means: dispose ourselves, purification, casting from ourselves the love of all creatures, going out of ourselves in detachment. These are phrases we find in the early works of our fathers in the Society of Jesus. The positive aspect is placing our love in the Creator of them all, entering into him, keeping a kind of particular examen [of conscience], having great courage and willingness to try, and having great faith and confidence that God will give us this grace.

As [Joseph] Aispun said, "finding God in all things" is not a method of prayer as we have in the case of meditation or contemplation or the application of senses. This experience is completely different. Finding God in all things presupposes a total death to the self. The death of the empirical self is the crowning glory of the Spiritual Exercises: that a person's self-love, self-will, and self-interest have merged into the will and the interest and the love of Christ. As long as we can live this for a few moments, for a few hours, for a few days, we have become contemplatives in action. So it is really a mystical grace. We cannot produce it, but we can dispose ourselves for it by loving God. We can seek him and we can ask for the grace, but we cannot really produce it.

[Francisco de] Villanueva wrote to the scholastics: "You say 'I am immersed in my studies all day, and when I go to prayer I find myself dry and the matter I have studied keeps coming to mind.'" He replied: "Our father Ignatius wants you to take your studies as prayer, directing them always and guiding them toward our Lord on whose service and for whose love *alone* you study, so that the end and the aim of all studies may be to please God and to do his holy will as manifested by the superior who commands you to study . . . and this will be easy for you if you don't take a liking for studies out of self-love or self-gratification."

Notice he does not say: "Don't take a liking for studies." He says not to take a liking for studies out of self-love and self-gratification, but *solely* because you seek to please God. He continues by warning scholastics that if this is all they seek without any admixture of self-love, they will be at ease, no matter where they are, whether studying or in the kitchen. If they want to take everything they do in this fashion, it will be like a prayer, and in prayer the Lord our God will give them great sentiments and consolations. Villanueva asks scholastics:

Do you want to find out whether you have studied for God alone? See if after you have studied you find yourself quiet, peaceful, and fervent without any remorse. If you do, it is a sign that you are studying only for God, for if your conscience is at peace, it is a sign that your soul is in its proper place and center . . . He who is indifferent and who would not study at all if it were not commanded him to do so, remains peaceful and happy, for he studies in the midst of continual prayer and his studies are themselves a prayer . . . The reason it proves an obstacle to prayer is the will is too attached to this study and so if you detach your will from it and you make yourself indifferent, you will find the remedy you are seeking in your question.

FINDING GOD IN APOSTOLIC ACTION

To find God in apostolic action is important for us Jesuits because we have an apostolic vocation. St. Teresa of Avila believed this holds true not only for people who have an apostolic vocation, but also for anybody who comes close to God. They have a great hunger to give God to others, to reach out and bring other people to God. Toward the end of her life she wrote:

> O treasure of my soul, there is a reason why, in the midst of all these great delights and these sweet joys which we experience in your company, we are afflicted. It is the thought of the great number of those who do not wish for these joys and will lose them for eternity. Hence it is that the soul strives to discover companions, and willingly leaves the happiness which inundates her, persuading others to see and share in her happiness. But would it not be better for her to postpone these desires for a time when she will be less showered with your caresses and devote herself entirely for the time being to enjoying them? O my Jesus, what is this great love which you bring to the sons of man? The most considerable service we can render you is to leave you for their love and their advantage. In that we possess you more fully. The will, it is true, is less intoxicated from your happiness, but the soul rejoices in making you content. She experiences the joys which we experience here below even though they are gifts from you, but they are uncertain during this mortal life if they are not accompanied by

love for the neighbor. Those who do not love their neighbor do not really love you.

Teresa is yearning to get away from Christ so that other people may have the joy that she has. St. Paul speaks of that tension, which he frames in the form of a dilemma: "If I am to live in the flesh, that means fruitful labor for me; and I do not know which I prefer. I am hard pressed between the two: my desire is to depart and be with Christ, for that is far better; but to remain in the flesh is more necessary for you. Since I am convinced of this, I know that I will remain and continue with all of you for your progress and joy in faith" (Phil. 1:22–24). The test of the prayer of an apostle is that the more he prays, the more he wants to get away from Christ and be with people and reassure them. The more he is with people, the more he is longing to get away and be with Christ.

What the *Imitation of Christ* says to me is 100 percent true, and yet only half of the truth. "Whenever I was with men, the less of a man I felt." We must understand what the author means. It is this tension. This idea is well expressed in the *Four Degrees of Passionate Charity* by Richard of St. Victor.

There are four degrees of passion to love of God. In the first degree God enters into the soul and she turns inward into herself. In the second she ascends above herself and is lifted up to God. In the third, the soul, lifted up to God, passes over into him, is transformed into him. The two of them become one. In the fourth she goes forth on God's behalf and descends below herself. In the first she enters in by meditation; in the second by contemplation; in the third she is led into jubilation; in the fourth she goes out by compassion. In the last stage the image of Christ is set before the soul so that these words come to her: "Let the same mind be in you that was in Christ Jesus, who, though he was in the form of God, did not regard equality with God as something to be exploited, but emptied himself, taking the form of a slave, being born in human likeness. And being found in human form, he humbled himself and became obedient to the point of death—even death on a cross" [Phil. 2:5–8]. This is the form of the humility of Christ to which people must conform themselves if they desire to attain the highest degree of perfect charity.

What is Richard saying? When you have been so transformed, you have become just like Jesus Christ. "No one has greater love than this, to lay down one's life for one's friends" (John 15:13). Jesus does not speak of "great love for man" but he is simply saying there is no greater love than this; that people lay down their lives. Love of what? Love of God, love of everything. Those who lay down their lives for their friends have reached the highest peak of charity; they have already reached the fourth degree of charity—passionate love of God. Even the third degree that Richard of St. Victor talks about the soul is in a way almost in the likeness of God—her substance has been changed into the substance of God, as St. John of the Cross says. Nevertheless, in the fourth degree, she begins to empty herself, takes the form of a servant and begins "being found in human form" (Phil. 2:7). This is very reminiscent of the Buddha's whole attitude: One sets out in search of illumination, becomes illuminated, and then is completely different. At the final stage people return and are humans like everyone else. It is what we call "return to the marketplace." We are the same as everyone else, but changed.

Another example is experiencing in the beginning that trees are trees and that mountains are mountains. Suddenly there are no more trees and no more mountains. We have been transformed. In the last stage, trees are trees once again, and mountains are once again mountains. We have become ordinary persons once more. What a difference, however, exists between the first stage and the third!

The love of the people who have this fourth degree of charity "bears all things, believes all things, hopes all things, endures all things" (1 Cor. 13:7). Such people desire to be banished from Christ for their brothers' and sisters' sake (Rom. 9:3). Is it not complete madness to reject true life, to refuse the highest wisdom, to resist omnipotence, and even desire to be separated from Christ for the sake of others? Is it not a rejection of true life? Consider the boldness of presuming that the perfection of charity can raise up the mind of people. Or, as we have said, in the first degree the soul enters into itself, in the second it attends to God, in the third it passes out into God, and in the fourth it descends below itself. This is how Jesus loved us. He "emptied himself" of his Godness for us. Now we empty ourselves of our God for the brethren.

To put this in concrete terms, I think that when people have a taste of God they fall in love with God. Something happens to them. They are suddenly pulled away and fall into a kind of sickness if the God experience is powerful enough. The sickness can be summarized as "Does anything else really matter?" Plato's *Republic* provides a nice comparison. There the whole of humanity is sitting facing the wall of a cave. The entrance is behind and a fire is burning behind with shadows projected on the wall. We look at these shadows and are taken up with them. At this point I will adapt the metaphor a bit. We have a mirror and on it are reflected images, reflected stars, reflected persons, and reflected reality. Now, Plato says that occasionally in the history of humanity we will find a person who is bold enough to turn around—it is forbidden to turn around—and who walks to the entrance of the cave. Reality returns. The person looks at the reflections and tries to convince everybody that these are reflections only. They want to kill this person who is upsetting their whole world.

Those who touch reality lose any appetite for life as humans know it. The others killed Socrates; they killed Jesus as they have killed the prophets who have disturbed their way of life. When people have tasted real water, why would they want to drink reflected water? When they have met real persons, why would they want to meet reflected persons? A sickness comes over them; they are sick of everything. This is the danger we face when we withdraw into ourselves: We want to abandon the world, to give it up as meaningless. I believe there is one thing that pulls people out of themselves and out of this sickness. The first step is to acknowledge that each one of us can experience such a sickness. This is a necessary stage in our spiritual growth and our growth as apostles. What can pull us out is compassion. If compassion enters people's hearts when they see other human beings deprived of this, compassion will pull them out of themselves. We can all extend compassion to other people.

Christians have another motive—a very powerful one—the love for Christ. If I can bring one more heart to Christ, if one more person can love Jesus, if Jesus would have the delight of being loved and known by one more person, if there is a personal relationship with Jesus Christ, then my desire for Jesus to have one more friend, the love of one more person, makes that person attractive and lovable. That is something I have experienced. When I have an intimate friend, I want him or her to love my other intimate friends. It distresses me if they do not love one another. When you love someone very deeply, you want that person to be loved by as many people as possible. That is what St. Teresa is talking about when she says she wants to share Christ with other people. That is the root of all apostolic activity. Other things can arise from critical parents, from an ideal, and from pushing ourselves, but until the heart has been touched and people have fallen into this sickness, the sickness of love, that apostolic zeal is not really apostolic zeal. It is living up to an ideal, it is giving yourself a good feeling that you are doing something worthwhile in life, but it is not what St. Paul speaks of when he writes, "For the love of Christ urges us on" (2 Cor. 5:14).

This love has two aspects. One aspect is this experience. In compassion and love, people go out to others and want to draw them to Christ. They do not wait for the fourth degree of love. The second aspect is realizing that the more people give Christ to others, the more they gain him. The more they share God's treasures with others, the more they grow in their own hearts. The more they grow in their own hearts, the greater is their desire to share with others. That is why when I give retreats to Jesuits I tell them at the end of the retreat that I do not believe that the renewal of the Society comes through long retreats. I have never had any illusions about the long-retreat movement. I believe that the total renewal of the Society will come the day when every Jesuit in his heart ardently desires to give Christ to others, to give God to others, to give the Spirit to others, to give spiritually to others, to bring people to the Absolute. When people have this attitude in their hearts, they can forget about long retreats and the rest of it, because the Spirit will come alive in each one's own heart. As soon as people start giving him to others, they come alive. They keep only what they share and what they give.

I would like to end this section with a quote from Albert Schweitzer (1875–1965) from his book *The Quest of the Historical Jesus*.

> He comes to us as one unknown, without a name, as of old by the lakeside. He comes to those men who knew him not. And he speaks to us the same words: "Follow me" and sets us to the tasks which he has to fulfill for our times. He commands, and to those who obey him, whether they be wise or simple, he will reveal himself in the toils, the sufferings, the conflicts which they shall pass through in his fellowship, and as an ineffable mystery they shall learn in their own experience who he is.

Allowing for Growth

In seeking God everywhere, we must allow for growth. A common problem is that we develop a mystical doctrine and want to put it into practice right now. Many people are not ready for it; they are not ready to die for others. We cannot produce it. What do we do? Wait, wait. This is a concept that never entered our Jesuit spirituality and formation.

Wait: The Holy Spirit is not getting through by our using spiritual muscles. The Spirit is getting through by our waiting. Jesus told his apostles: "[S]tay here in the city [Jerusalem] until you have been clothed with power from on high" (Luke 24:49). The power will come from above. In the meantime we must grow and be patient.

What happens in the early stages of human life? The child cannot give love; the child needs to receive love. That is what is happening to us, since so many of us are still children. We need to look after the child in us; we need to give ourselves the love we have been deprived of for so many years. Unless we realize that, we will jump into love with others in a forced and strained way. If I sacrifice myself for others, that is the most pernicious thing I can do because there is a subtle pride in that; there is a kind of resentment. I am not a cheerful giver. I am tinged with guilt, with an ideal. In reality, I do not love you; I love the ideal. When our needs are met and we have grown, the tree bears fruit. Love comes spontaneously; we do not produce it. George Soares said to us once: "The New Testament is against good works. Christ did not say 'I am sending you out to do good works,' but said 'I am sending you out to bear fruit.'" Fruit is the work of divine grace, not of our own efforts. We grow. We take in the Holy Spirit. We can discover who is or who is not spiritually mature, when we find out that the Spirit has stopped working in that person.

Parmananda [Divarkar] put it well several years ago: Mary begins almost where St. Paul ends. Paul asked: "What do you want me to do?" Mary replied: "Let it be done to me according to your will." A great maturity is present in both these people, as well as surrender, peace, life, and allowing the Spirit to do everything. Insecurity drops. I urge you to grow, but do not produce. Let the Spirit work. Stop straining your spiritual muscles. Become attuned to your deeper self and let the force of life take over. Let the Holy Spirit take over. Instead of setting forth propositions that we must attain, let them be like milestones that tell us where we are. Then a time will come when it will be personally delightful to die for a friend. It will not be a sacrifice, and, let us hope that we will do this for everyone.

NOTES

Chapter One: First Principle and Foundation

1. **"Man cannot be happy for long unless . . .":** Thomas Merton, *The Silent Life* (New York: Farrar, Straus & Giroux, 1957), pp. 166–67.

2. **"We are frequently cast out from our hearts . . .":** Congregation of Monk Hermits of Camaldoli, a religious order founded in the eleventh century as a reformed community of Benedictines.

2. **"If you love truth, be a lover of silence . . .":** Thomas Merton, *Contemplative Prayer* (New York: Herder and Herder, 1969), pp. 33–34.

2. **"Behold my beloved . . .":** "Letter 12," *Patrologia Orientalis* 11, 606. This quotation also appears in Merton, *Contemplative Prayer*, p. 50.

2. **"You talk when you cease to be at peace . . .":** Kahlil Gibran, *The Prophet* (New York: Knopf, 1951), p. 60.

3. **"the self is yet unacquainted with the strange claim of silence . . .":** Evelyn Underhill, *Mysticism: A Study in Nature and Development of Spiritual Consciousness* (Grand

Rapids, MI: Christian Classics Ethereal Library, 2003), p. 227.

3. **"At times the first words . . .":** Simone Weil, *Waiting for God* (New York: Harper Colophon Books, 1951), p. 72.

5. **Louis Evely:** A Christian spiritual writer and evangelist from Belgium.

6. **when he was a regent . . . :** "Regency" is the two- or three-year period in a Jesuit's formation when he is engaged in some active apostolate, usually between his philosophical and theological studies.

7. **Rishi:** A rishi is an author of Vedic hymns who is regarded as a combination of a patriarch, a priest, and a preceptor.

7. *The Intimate Enemy:* George Robert Bach, *The Intimate Enemy* (New York: Avon Books, 1968).

8. **Charles de Foucauld:** Charles de Foucauld (1858–1916) inspired several associations of the faithful, religious communities and secular institutes for both laypeople and priests. He was beatified by Pope Benedict XVI in 2005.

8. **"When I came to know that God exists . . .":** Michael Carrouges, *Soldier of the Spirit: The Life of Charles de Foucauld* (New York: G. P. Putnam's Sons, 1956), p. 86.

8. **"We shall be detached from all ideas by banishing every memory . . .":** Here de Mello refers to a collection of writings found in Charles de Foucauld, *Meditations of a Hermit,* trans. Charlotte Balfour (1930; repr., London: Burns & Oates, 1981), pp. 36–41, 165, 167.

8. **Teilhard:** Pierre Teilhard de Chardin (1881–1955) was a Jesuit priest, paleontologist, biologist, and philosopher. He spent the bulk of his life trying to integrate religious experience with natural science, most specifically Christian theology with theories of evolution.

12. **"I must serve my fellowmen . . .":** From *The Collected Works of Mahatma Gandhi*, vol. 63 (Ahmedabad: Navajivan Trust, 1976), p. 240.

17. **by the middle of the second week it is to be hoped that they will understand it . . . :** Sometimes de Mello seems to suggest that the retreatant will reach his goal in the second week. This can sound a little like a traditional view for which the third and fourth weeks are only a "confirmation" or "the icing on the cake."

Chapter Two: Our Sinfulness

22. **Unless we feel the need for God . . . :** Ignatius tells the retreatant at the beginning of the *Exercises* that he should "enter upon them with magnanimity and generosity toward his Creator and Lord, and to offer him his entire will and liberty, that his Divine Majesty may dispose of him and all he possesses according to his most holy will" (no. 5). That same attitude should prevail at the end: "Take, Lord, and receive all my liberty, my memory, my understanding, and my entire will, all that I have and possess. Thou hast given all to me. To thee, O Lord, I return it. All is thine, dispose of it wholly according to thy will. Give me thy love and thy grace, for this is sufficient for me" (no. 234).

22. **But this is only one aspect of the grace of repentance . . . :** De Mello believed that "[a]lthough sin is something that has to be regretted and detested, it is not something for which we must hate ourselves or something for which I am frightened. The first week and the contemplation of sin is a contemplation for great rejoicing and love, instead of being a week when people are all depressed and discouraged, hate themselves more, and become gloomy."

25. **Luke 13:1–5:** "At that very time there were some present who told him about the Galileans whose blood Pilate

had mingled with their sacrifices. He asked them, 'Do you think that because these Galileans suffered in this way they were worse sinners than all other Galileans? No, I tell you; but unless you repent, you will all perish as they did. Or those eighteen who were killed when the tower of Siloam fell on them—do you think that they were worse offenders than all the others living in Jerusalem? No, I tell you; but unless you repent, you will all perish just as they did.'"

25. **Blaise Pascal:** Blaise Pascal (1623–1662), French mathematician and apologist.

31. **Or look to Origen . . . :** The Second Council of Constantinople (553) condemned the teachings of Origen about universal salvation and other matters.

32. *Prayers*: Michel Quoist, *Prayers* (New York: Sheed and Ward, 1963).

33. **Ramdas:** Ramdas (1884–1963), born in Kerala, left his home, his wife, and his children in 1922 in order to live the life of a sadhu (ascetic or practitioner of yoga), unconcerned about where he was going or what would happen, living every moment with the Ram Mantra continually on his lips and the love of God in his heart. He spread a message of religious unity and the magnificence of the One Almighty Lord throughout India and around the world.

Chapter Three: Repentance

37. **Tears form one of the gifts . . . :** "The third reason is because God wishes to give us a true knowledge and understanding of ourselves, so that we may have an intimate perception of the fact that it is not within our power to acquire and attain great devotion, intense love, tears, or any other spiritual consolation; but that all this is the gift and grace of God our Lord" (no. 322).

37. **sadhu:** A sadhu is a Hindu ascetic, a monk.

38. **William Barclay:** William Barclay (1907–1978) was a New Testament scholar who taught at the University of Glasgow and excelled at communicating the Scriptures to a wide public.

39. **"O Lord, our God, give us the grace . . .":** In *The Double-day Prayer Collection*, comp. Mary Batchelor (New York: Doubleday, 1996), p. 11.

41. **[Pedro] Arrupe:** Pedro Arrupe (1907–1991) was superior general of the Society of Jesus from 1965 to 1983.

42. **[Ignacio] Casanovas:** Ignacio Casanovas (1872–1936), a Spanish writer on spirituality, was on the staff of the periodical *Razón y Fé* and is famous for his biography of St. Ignatius Loyola.

44. **Aldous Huxley:** Aldous Huxley (1894–1963) was an English novelist and essayist who is best known for his 1932 work about the future, *Brave New World*.

48. **"Do everything as if everything depends . . .":** This saying is treated in J. B. Libânio, "St. Ignatius and Liberation," *The Way*, Supplement 70 (Spring 1991): 51–63 at p. 56, along with its accompanying endnote.

48. **See what Ignatius says in no. 53:** "Imagine Christ our Lord present before you upon the cross, and begin to speak with him, asking how it is that though he is the creator, he has stooped to become man, and to pass from eternal life to death here in time, that thus he might die for our sins.

    "I shall also reflect upon myself and ask:

    " 'What have I done for Christ?'

    " 'What am I doing for Christ?'

    " 'What ought I to do for Christ?'

    "As I behold Christ in this plight, nailed to the cross, I shall ponder upon what presents itself to my mind" (no. 53).

48. **the prayer of simplicity:** Alphonsus Liguori, *Homo Apostolicus*, Appendix I, No. 7 cited at www.newadvent.org.

51. **St. Margaret Mary Alacoque:** Although the several "promises" made to St. Margaret Mary are not put in one place, one might consult George Tickell, *The Life of Blessed Margaret Mary* (New York: P. J. Kennedy & Sons, 1890), p. 296. A more up-to-date version is that of Mary Fabyan Windeatt, *Mission for Margaret* (St. Meinrad, Indiana: Grail, 1953), p. 102.

Chapter Four: The Kingdom of Christ

55. **Jesus always told his disciples that to suffer and to die is necessary. But he never said a single word to explain why:** These last two statements call for qualifications. (1) At times the Gospels portray Jesus as speaking of his coming suffering and death but without saying that it was "necessary": for instance, Mark 9:31; 10:33–34. (2) At times the Gospels portray Jesus as providing an "explanation" for his own suffering: for instance, Mark 10:45; Matthew 26:28; John 12:24–25. (3) At times the Gospels portray Jesus as providing grounds for the suffering of his followers: their reward will be "great in heaven" (Luke 6:23).

56. **Bonhoeffer says that when Christ calls a person . . . :** Dietrich Bonhoeffer, *Cost of Discipleship* (New York: Macmillan, 1964), p. 79.

57. **We could read all the works of Karl Rahner . . . :** See Philip Endean, *Karl Rahner and Ignatian Spirituality* (Oxford: Oxford University Press, 2004).

58. **"The cross is sweet . . .":** José Calveras, *The Harvest-field of the Spiritual Exercises of Saint Ignatius* (Bombay: St. Xavier College, 1949). See chapter 3, n. 8.

59. **Fritz Perls:** Fritz Perls, a noted psychiatrist and psychotherapist, coined the term "Gestalt therapy" in the 1940s.

59. **"If one accepts all these hardships . . .":** Henry Coleridge, *The Life and Letters of St. Francis Xavier*, vol. 1 (New York: Benziger Brothers, 1902), p. 121.

61. **the third degree of humility:** According to the *Exercises*, "[The third kind of humility] is the most perfect kind of humility. It consists in this. If we suppose the first and second kind attained, then whenever the praise and glory of the Divine Majesty would be equally served, in order to imitate and be in reality more like Christ our Lord, I desire and choose poverty with Christ poor, rather than riches; insults with Christ loaded with them, rather than honors; I desire to be accounted as worthless and a fool for Christ, rather than to be esteemed as wise and prudent in this world. So Christ was treated before me" (no. 167).

64. **The imagination is key:** A good explanation of the role of imagination is found in no. 47: "When the contemplation or meditation is on something visible, for example, when we contemplate Christ our Lord, the representation will consist in seeing in imagination the material place where the object is that we wish to contemplate. I said the material place, for example, the temple, or the mountain where Jesus or his mother is, according to the subject matter of the contemplation.

"In a case where the subject matter is not visible, as . . . in a meditation on sin, the representation will be to see in imagination my soul as a prisoner in this corruptible body, and to consider my whole composite being as an exile here on earth, cast out to live among brute beasts. I say my whole composite being, body and soul."

67. **"What do I love when I love my God? . . .":** Augustine, *Confessions* 10.6.8.

67. **"It happens sometimes that the Lord . . .":** These two passages come from a letter that Ignatius wrote in 1536

to Teresa Rejadell (in Barcelona). The passages are better translated in J. A. Munitiz and P. Endean, *Saint Ignatius Loyola: Personal Writings* (London: Penguin, 1996), pp. 133–134.

70. **"You know my love for you . . .":** This refers to a July 28, 1925, speech that Gandhi gave at the YMCA in Calcutta to young Christian missionaries (cf. *Collected Works of Mahatma Gandhi*, vol. 27 [Ahmedabad: Navajivan Press, 1968], pp. 434–41). E. Stanley Jones recounts it in *Gandhi: Portrayal of a Friend* (Nashville: Abdingdon Press, 1948), p. 60.

71. **"I appreciate the love . . .":** In Jones, *Portrayal of a Friend*, p. 60.

72. **"That woman said":** *Autobiography of St. Ignatius Loyola*, translated by Joseph O'Callaghan, introduction and notes by John Olin (New York: Harper & Row, 1974), p. 34.

73. **"I did not learn what I know from any man":** Cf. *Autobiography*, pp. 37–40.

Chapter Five: Being Interiorly Free: "The Three Classes of People"

74. **"Three Classes of People":** "This is a meditation to choose that which is better" (no. 149).

80. **[Pedro] de Ribadeneira:** Pedro de Ribadeneira (1526–1611) wrote a life of St. Ignatius Loyola, much as an eyewitness.

81. **[Gian Pietro] Caraffa:** as Pope Paul IV from 1555 to 1559.

81. **a "coincidence of opposites" . . . :** Cardinal Nicholas of Cusa (1401–1464) in his *De Docta Ignorantia* (completed 1440) defended the "coincidence of opposites." This is an approach for which the ineffability of the Infinite coincides with its expressibility, in which creation coin-

cides with creator, and transcendent coincides with immanent.

Chapter Six: "Elections"—Making Life Decisions

93. **Ignatius's remark about not "giving cause" for such humiliations . . . :** This phrase is found in the *Constitutions of the Society of Jesus*, chapter 4, which specifies observances to be followed within the Society.

93. **Joseph Rickaby:** Joseph Rickaby (1845–1932) was a nineteenth-century Jesuit writer and commentator on the Exercises.

93. **when the blind stirring of love begins . . . :** These ideas are found in chapters 26 and 34 of a fourteenth-century work written by an anonymous author, upon which the theology of centering prayer is based.

Chapter Seven: Discernment of Spirits

101. **"Just as the bee is led by instinct . . .":** This is covered in St. Thomas Aquinas, *De Anima*, 3, 5.

101. **"In matters of great moment . . .":** Pedro Ribadeneira, "Fontes Narrativi III," *Monumenta Historica Societatis Iesu*, vol. 85 (Rome: Monumenta Historica Societatis Iesu, 1960), p. 569.

108. **"The more I see myself . . .":** St. Ignatius Loyola, "Letter to Francis Borgia, Duke of Gandia, 1545," *Letters of St. Ignatius Loyola*, William J. Young, ed. (Chicago: Loyola University Press, 1959), pp. 84–85.

109. **a kind of Pelagian attitude . . . :** A monk from the British Isles who lived around 400, Pelagius went to Rome and then North Africa. He taught that human beings can achieve salvation through their own sustained efforts.

110. **"Knowing within ourselves . . .":** St. Ignatius Loyola, "Letter to Francis Borgia, Duke of Gandia, 1548," p. 181.

110. **Vinoba Bhave:** Vinoba Bhave (1895–1982) is often considered a teacher of India and the spiritual successor of Mahatma Gandhi.

114. **a tertian:** A tertian is someone who is in the last year of spiritual formation as a Jesuit.

121. **the foundress of the Maryknoll Sisters:** Mother Mary Joseph Rogers (1882–1955).

126. **"Let them all advance in true virtue . . .":** George Ganss, ed., *The Constitutions of the Society of Jesus* (St. Louis: Institute of Jesuit Sources, 1970), no. 260.

126. **"I cannot believe that anyone . . .":** This is found in St. Teresa's autobiography (*Life*), chapter 11. See also Teresa's *Way of Perfection*, chapter 17, no. 7 and *Interior Castle*, "The Fourth Dwelling Places," chapter 2, no. 10.

133. **Father Maurice Giuliani:** Father Maurice Giuliani (1916–2003), who served for seven years as assistant to Father Pedro Arrupe, Superior General of the Society of Jesus, founded the French Review *Christus* to bring about a renewal of Ignatian spirituality.

137. **Vishnu:** Vishnu is a form of God in Hinduism.

Chapter Eight: The Third and Fourth Weeks

139. **Ramanarshi:** Usually called Sri Ramana Maharshi (1879–1950), he was an Indian sage who was known for his teachings about self-inquiry.

143. **bhakti:** *Bhakti* is a Hindu term that denotes the spiritual practice of fostering loving devotion to a personal form of God.

144. **[Karl] Rahner:** Karl Rahner was a very prominent German Jesuit theologian.

148. **Walking in the newness of life . . . :** Harvey Cox, *God's Revolution and Man's Responsibility* (Valley Forge, Penn.: Judson Press, 1965), p. 94.

149. **"Man is challenged to participate . . .":** Dietrich Bonhoeffer, *Prisoner for God* (New York: Macmillan Co., 1953), pp. 166–67.

149. **"To be a Christian means to be a human being . . .":** Bonhoeffer, ibid.

150. **"But there was not going to be a next time for Bonhoeffer . . .":** Ibid., p. 99. In this paragraph Cox is quoting from Dietrich Bonhoeffer's *Prisoner for God* (New York: Macmillan Co., 1953), pp. 166–67.

150. **She sees Jesus hanging right merrily . . . :** The works of Julian of Norwich are written in "old" English. Everything we have is a translation or a paraphrase. This particular reference can be found at: Julian of Norwich, *Showing*, eds. Edmund Colledge and James Walsh (New York: Paulist, 1978), p. 138.

153. **Bernanos:** Georges Bernanos (1888–1948) was a French writer.

153. **Anthony Bloom:** Anthony Bloom (1914–2003) was a Metropolitan in the Russian Orthodox Church and a writer.

154. **"My acquaintance with Christianity . . .":** Here de Mello synopsizes the material found in Anthony Bloom, *Beginning to Pray* (New York: Paulist Press, 1970), p. xii.

155. **Jean Vanier:** Born in 1928, Jean Vanier founded the L'Arche (Ark) movement in France in 1964 to bring together people with developmental disabilities. Volunteers live in homes with them and help all realize their unique values and gifts. The L'Arche movement has spread all over the world.

Chapter Nine: Contemplation to Attain the Love of God

159. **"the whole of my being . . .":** St. John of the Cross, *Spiritual Canticle II*, ed. and trans. Antonio de Nicolás (New York: Paragon House, 1989), p. 125.

159. **To serve God means to do God's will . . . :** This is a paraphrase of No. 280 and No. 281 of the Jesuit *Constitutions*.

159. **"All should have a right intention . . .":** Jesuit *Constitutions*, Part VIII, chapter 1, no. 288.

165. **Parmananda:** Father Parmananda Divarkar, S.J., who was an authority on Ignatian spirituality, served in Rome as a general assistant to the Jesuit superior general from 1975 to 1983.

166. **we are so gripped by this power . . . :** *The Cloud of Unknowing*, chapter 26; see also chapter 34.

167. **nishkam karma, "selfless action":** *Nishkam karma*, or "selfless action," is so named because it is considered to be an action that is performed without any expectation of fruits or reward whatsoever.

168. **"In our era the path to holiness . . . :** Dag Hammarskjöld, *Markings* (New York: Knopf, 1968), pp. xxi, 122.

169. **"The aim of their studies . . .":** "Letter to Father Antonio Brandao" in *Letters of St. Ignatius of Loyola*, William J. Young, ed. (Chicago: Loyola University Press, 1959), p. 240. This matter is also covered in George Ganss, ed., *The Constitutions of the Society of Jesus* (St. Louis: Institute of Jesuit Sources, 1970), nos. 340, 360, 361.

169. **"And this manner of meditation . . .":** Ibid.

170. **"So briefly, in all our works we must find peace . . .":** For a discussion of contemplative in action see W. V. Bangert and T. M. McCoog, *Jerome Nadal, S.J. 1507–1580. Tracking the First Generation of Jesuits* (Chicago: Loyola University Press, 1992), pp. 214–15. The expression *"contemplativus in actione"* is used by Nadal only once, and that in the fourth volume of his works, speaking of St. Ignatius. But in different places he speaks of St. Ignatius as one who "was able to *find God in all things*." This is the basis for the Society to accept the traditional in-

terpretation of Nadal's expression. See Miguel Nicolau, *Jerome Nadal (1507–1580): Obras y Doctrinas Espirituales* (Madrid: Consejo Superior de Investigaciones Cientificas, 1949).

172. **Aispun:** Joseph Aispun, Indian Jesuit and friend of de Mello.

172. **"You say 'I am immersed in my studies . . .'":** Francisco de Villanueva (1509–1557) was one of the most notable directors in the first generation of Jesuits. He explained how he understood the giving of the Exercises as a ministry of gentle support within an attitude of radical respect for the exercitant's freedom. See his "Letter to a Former Retreatant," *The Way* 45, no. 1 (January 2006): 33–37, and the biography of Villanueva provided there.

174. **O treasure of my soul . . . :** St. Teresa of Avila, "Exclamations of the Soul to God," II. This is de Mello's translation of the Spanish. An English translation can be found at E. Allison Peers, *The Complete Works of Saint Teresa of Jesus*, vol. 2 (New York: Sheed and Ward, 1946), p. 403.

175. **"Whenever I was with men . . .":** Thomas à Kempis, *Imitation of Christ*, 1.20.

175. **"There are four degrees of passion" . . . :** This loose translation and synopsis is from Richard of St. Victor, *Of Four Degrees of Passionate Charity, Selected Writings on Contemplation*, trans. Clare Kirchberger (London: Faber and Faber, 1957), pp. 215–35, especially at pp. 224 and 230.

176. **When you have been so transformed . . . :** The "self-emptying" of which Paul writes in Philippians 2:9 does *not* mean that in the Incarnation the Son of God literally divested himself of his divinity and ceased to be divine. It is rather a question of his lovingly accepting the self-limitation involved in his taking on the human condition

in a situation that led to his horrendous death on the cross. See G. O'Collins, *Incarnation* (London/New York: Continuum, 2002), pp. 58–64.

180. **"He comes to us as one unknown . . .":** Albert Schweitzer, *The Quest of the Historical Jesus* (1968; repr., Baltimore: Johns Hopkins Press, 1998), p. 403.

181. **George Soares:** George M. Soares-Prabhu (1929–1995), an Indian Jesuit writer.

INDEX OF NAMES

ANTHONY DE MELLO, S.J., was the director of the Sadhana Institute of Pastoral Counseling in Pune, India. A member of the Jesuit province of Bombay (Mumbai), he was known throughout the world for his writings and spiritual conferences. Although he died suddenly in 1987, through his many books, including *Awareness*, *Sadhana*, and *The Song of the Bird*, which have been translated into more than thirty-five languages, he leaves a rich legacy of spiritual teaching.